What Do I Do With My Hands?

FROM AWKWARD TO AWESOME

A Photographer's Guide to
Hand Posing

Amanda Otis

What Do I Do With My Hands?
From Awkward to Awesome

A Photographer's Guide to Hand Posing

AMANDA OTIS

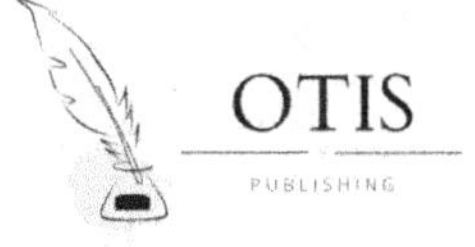

Contents

Introduction

Have you ever been in the middle of a photoshoot, everything is going perfectly, the lighting is just right, the backdrop is a photographer's dream, and then... your subject looks at you with a mix of confusion and mild panic and mutters, "What do I do with my hands?" Ah, the universal riddle that photographers and their subjects have been trying to solve since the dawn of the camera. It's a question that can stump the most experienced among us, turning a confident shoot into an awkward dance of hand placement. This, my friends, is where our journey begins.

Welcome to "What Do I Do With My Hands?" not just another posing guide but your ultimate companion in answering this very common question. This book isn't just about telling your subjects where to put their hands; it's about opening up a whole new dialogue of creative communication between photographer and subject.

Let me share a little story. Once upon a shoot, I found myself with a subject who was a natural in front of the camera, except for one tiny thing—their hands. They were stiff, awkward, and just plain lost. It was that moment, amidst the silent cries for help from those two hands, that I realized the power of guiding with purpose. And thus, the seed for this book was planted.

Our goal here is simple yet profound: to arm you, dear photographers, with a repertoire of hand poses and the strategies to communicate them, boosting your confidence and that of your subjects. This isn't just about making pictures look good; it's about elevating the entire photographic experience, ensuring that confidence radiates from both sides of the camera.

Whether you're a beginner just starting to explore the world of photography, a seasoned professional looking to add new layers to your work, or a photography student eager to absorb every piece of knowledge, this book is for you. And it's not just for photographers. Models, actors, and anyone interested in the subtle art of body language in photos will find invaluable insights within these pages.

Expect a ride through an engaging, conversational tone packed with practical advice, professional insights, and, yes, a healthy dose of humor. We'll break down complex concepts into bite- sized, accessible pieces, ensuring you're not just reading, but enjoying and learning every step of the way.

Structured to cover everything from the fundamentals to creative posing ideas across various genres, common challenges, advanced techniques, and the cultural nuances of hand posing, this book promises a comprehensive look at the art (dare I say science) of hand placement. And yes, it's going to be a visual feast too, with high-quality images showcasing a diverse range of styles, subjects, and settings to inspire and guide you.

But that's not all. We're living in a digital age, after all. You'll find QR codes sprinkled throughout, linking you to tutorials and demonstrations to enrich your learning experience and ensure that theory translates into practice.

So, consider this your invitation to join me on a transformative journey. Open your mind and be ready to change the way you approach hand posing in photography forever. And remember, with practice and the guidance nestled within these pages, mastering the nuances of hand posing is within your grasp (pun intended).

I'm thrilled to be part of your journey and can't wait to see where it takes you. Together, let's unlock the secrets of hand posing and elevate your photography to levels you've only dreamed of. Ready to get started? Let's turn the page and dive in.

Chapter 1: The Basics of Hand Posing

So, you've got your camera, your subject is beaming with excitement, and you're ready to capture some magic. But then, the age-old question pops up, "What do I do with my hands?" Suddenly, the room's energy shifts and those once eager hands hang awkwardly by their sides. Fear not! This chapter is your first step in conquering the mysterious world of hand posing. Here, we'll start with the basics, peel back the layers of hand psychology in portraits, and set you up with the tools to turn those awkward pauses into poignant expressions.

Breaking Down the Psychology of Hands in Portraiture

Ever noticed how a slight change in hand position can tell a completely different story? That's because hands are incredibly expressive tools that can convey a wide array of emotions and messages, often without us even realizing it. Let's unpack this, shall we?

The Power of Subconscious Signals

Hands are like the human psyche's unwitting accomplices, often giving away clues about our inner state that we might not voice out loud. For instance, clenched fists often signal tension or defiance, while open palms can suggest openness and honesty. This subconscious communication can give viewers a deeper insight into the subject's personality, enhancing the emotional depth of your portraits. Think about the last time you saw a photo where someone's hands were tightly clasped. Did you feel their anxiety? That's the power of subconscious signaling at play!

Hands as a Focal Point

But hands don't just hang around telling tales of our emotional states; they can also steal the spotlight in a portrait. By intentionally positioning hands, you can draw attention to specific aspects of the portrait or even highlight other elements of the story you're trying to tell. For example, a mother's gentle hand on her child's back can emphasize a sense of nurturing care. Hands can frame a face, guide the viewer's eye through the picture, or even be the main subject of the portrait itself. They're versatile like that!

Cultural Significance and Perception

Now, let's talk culture. Hand gestures can mean a myriad of things in different cultures. A thumbs-up in one country might be a positive affirmation, while in others, it could be a highly offensive gesture. When you're capturing hands, consider the cultural context and how it might interpret these hand signs. This awareness not only prevents potential faux pas but also enriches your portraits with a layer of cultural depth that can resonate more profoundly with a diverse audience.

Psychological Comfort and Discomfort

Finally, the way a subject positions their hands can tell you a lot about their comfort level during the shoot. Are their hands stiffly by their sides? They might be nervous. Are they playing absentmindedly with their hair? Perhaps they're feeling a bit self-conscious. Recognizing these signs allows you as the photographer to adjust your approach. Maybe you crack a joke to ease the mood, or perhaps you give them something to hold — a prop, perhaps? Monitoring and responding to the comfort levels indicated by hand placement can drastically improve the outcome of your portraits.

By understanding these psychological nuances, you're not just capturing images; you're capturing emotions, stories, and a bit of human soul. And that, dear reader, is what takes a good portrait to the realms of greatness. So next time you pick up your camera, remember, it's not just about where the hands are, but what they tell you. Keep your eyes open and your mind even more so.

Anatomy 101: Understanding Hand Movements and Limitations

Alright, let's roll up our sleeves—or maybe just flex our fingers—and dive into the fascinating world of hand anatomy. Understanding the nuts and bolts of how hands work isn't just for doctors and anatomists; it's crucial for us photographers too. After all, knowing what makes those hands tick, bend, and snap can be the difference between a pose that looks like a natural extension of the body and one that screams, "I'm so uncomfortable, please let this be over!" So, let's get a grip on the basics of joint flexibility, bone structure, muscle engagement, and how age plays into all of this.

Joint Flexibility and Limitation

First up, let's talk about joint flexibility. Each hand has 27 bones—yes, 27! That's a lot of moving parts, literally. These bones are connected by joints and ligaments allowing a broad range of motion. However, not all hands can perform the same magic tricks. Some folks can bend their fingers back to touch their wrist (please don't try this if you haven't done it before), while others might struggle to make a decent fist. As a photographer, understanding these natural limits is key to guiding your subjects into poses that they can achieve comfortably. Imagine asking someone who can barely wave properly to mimic a complex hand gesture from a classical painting—it's not going to end well. When positioning hands, observe how the subject moves their fingers and palms naturally, and use that as a baseline to build your pose. This approach not only prevents any strained ligaments but also keeps your models from feeling like they're in a hand-twisting boot camp.

Impact of Bone Structure on Posing

Moving on to the scaffolding of the hand: the bone structure. Just like faces, every hand has its unique bone structure that affects how poses look. Some people have long, slender fingers that can make elegant lines and shapes, perfect for those dreamy, soft-focus shots. Others have shorter, sturdier fingers that lend a sense of strength and solidity to images. Here's where your keen eye for detail comes into play. Notice the structure of your subject's hands and think about how you can best use their natural form to enhance your composition. For instance, longer fingers might elegantly drape over a chair's armrest, while stronger hands could be more impactful gripping a rugged tool or sports equipment. Adapting your pose to the individual's bone structure not only ensures comfort but also complements the overall aesthetic of your shot.

Muscle Engagement

Now, let's flex some muscle—literally. The hands are powered by a variety of muscles responsible for all those intricate movements we take for granted. From a gentle fingertip touch to a tight, dynamic fist, the muscles in the hand can convey a wide range of tension and emotion. As photographers, our job is to capture this dynamic interplay. A relaxed hand with lightly curled fingers can evoke calmness and serenity, while a clenched fist might channel intensity or aggression. Watch how your subject's muscles engage as they move their hands, and use this to your advantage. Encourage them to show the muscle tension that matches the shoot's mood. Is it a high-energy sports ad? Let those forearm and hand muscles pop. A serene bridal portrait? Keep the hands soft and lightly curved.

Age and Hand Anatomy

Finally, let's talk about age. Younger hands and older hands tell very different stories. A child's smooth, supple hands can symbolize innocence and potential, while an elder's weathered, lined hands can tell tales of wisdom and a well-lived life. When posing hands, consider the age of your subject and what their hands might convey about their life journey. For younger subjects, you might opt for poses that emphasize openness and vitality, like reaching towards the sky or gently holding a blossoming flower. For older subjects, consider poses that highlight the texture and contours of their hands, perhaps resting on a favorite walking stick or tenderly holding a family photo. By aligning your hand poses with the age-related characteristics of your subject, you not only enhance the authenticity of your portraits but also pay homage to the unique beauty found in every stage of life.

Understanding the anatomy of the hand in such depth allows you as a photographer to fully appreciate and utilize the expressive power of hands in your portraits. It's about making every finger count, every joint bend with purpose, and respecting the natural limits while pushing the creative boundaries. So next time you're framing a shot, take a moment to really see the hands, to understand what they can do and how they can best convey the essence of your subject.

With this knowledge, you're well on your way to mastering the subtle art of hand posing, one graceful gesture at a time.

The Language of Hands: Conveying Emotions Through Gestures

Imagine you're at a bustling coffee shop, trying to catch the eye of someone at the other end of the room. What do you do? A subtle wave, a polite hand raise, maybe a cheeky finger-gun if you're feeling adventurous. It's fascinating, isn't it, how our hands can speak volumes without uttering a single word? This is the essence we aim to capture in photography. Hands can articulate a spectrum of emotions, from seething anger to tender affection, all with just a flick, twist, or clasp. Let's dive into how these silent communicators work their magic in our visual stories.

Gestures as Emotional Expressions

Consider how a clenched fist can evoke feelings of resistance or combativeness, while a softly cupped face might convey intimacy or vulnerability. These are not just random movements; they're a language in themselves. For instance, think about capturing the raw energy of a protest. A photo where the subjects' hands are raised in unison, fists clenched, doesn't just show a group of people; it screams defiance and unity against a cause. On the flip side, imagine a quiet scene where a grandmother cradles her newborn grandchild with hands as delicate and detailed as a road map. Here, her hands speak of generations, of love, continuity, and protection. As photographers, our job is to recognize these powerful expressions and frame them in ways that amplify the intended emotion of the portrait.

Subtlety in Gesture

Now, while it's tempting to go all out and have hands dramatically flailing about to show emotion, there's something to be said for subtlety. It's like seasoning food; just the right amount can perfect a dish, but too much can overpower it. A slight touch, a gentle hold, or even a relaxed drape can often convey more depth than the most elaborate gesture. For example, during a couple's shoot, instead of having them hold hands in the usual interlocked style, why not try a gentle touch of the fingertips? It can suggest a budding romance, a delicate yet profound connection that's just starting to bloom. This type of subtlety can draw the viewer in, inviting them to look closer and really feel the emotion being conveyed.

Contextualizing Hand Gestures

Context is crucial when it comes to interpreting hand gestures. The same gesture can mean different things depending on where, when, and how it's used. Take the 'V' sign made with fingers; it's a peace sign in some parts of the world and a rude gesture in others. As photographers, being aware of the cultural and situational contexts of our subjects helps prevent miscommunication and enhances the relatability of the images. For instance, a hand placed over the heart in a portrait of an athlete can signify pride and love for their country, especially if captured during a national anthem at an international event.

Without understanding the context, viewers might interpret the gesture differently.

Hands in Interaction

Finally, the interaction between hands or between hands and other elements can narrate compelling relationships and stories. Picture this: a child learning to play the guitar, their tiny, unsure fingers guided by the more experienced, calloused hands of a loving parent. Here, the hands show a bond and tell a story of learning, of passing down knowledge and passion from one generation to another. Or consider a scene where a baker's hands, dusted with flour, are captured kneading dough. The interaction between hand and dough brings out textures and details, highlighting the craftsmanship and the tactile nature of the baking process.

By mastering the language of hands, you unlock a new dimension of storytelling in your photography. It's about seeing beyond the obvious, capturing the whispers of the hands, and letting them echo loudly in your frames. So next time you're out with your camera, watch the hands; they might just be the most expressive part of your next great photo.

Mastering the Art of Natural Hand Placement

Now that you've got a handle on the emotional and anatomical insights of hands, let's roll up our sleeves and get into the nitty-gritty of placing those hands in a way that feels as natural as laughing at a dad joke. You know, something that just comes without forced effort. The key to mastering hand placement isn't just about avoiding that deer-in-headlights look, but about creating a scene that whispers authenticity and speaks volumes in subtlety.

Guidelines for Natural Poses

First things first, let's lay down some ground rules for positioning hands in a way that doesn't scream "I was told to put my hand here," because nothing kills the vibe like an awkward hand hover. One of the simplest yet most effective guidelines is to mimic natural resting positions. Think about where your hands naturally fall when you're relaxed. Maybe it's lightly on your lap, or perhaps gently holding a cup of coffee. These are the sorts of relaxed positions you want to aim for in your shoots. Encourage your subjects to imagine holding something beloved or performing a light task—like tucking a strand of hair behind the ear or adjusting a pair of glasses. It's all about creating a scenario where the hands have a 'reason' to be where they are, rather than just floating in mid-air with no purpose.

The Role of Asymmetry

Moving on, let's chat about asymmetry. If you've ever looked at a photo and felt dynamically drawn to it, chances are, there was some clever use of asymmetry at play. When it comes to hand placement, asymmetry can be your best friend. It adds a layer of interest and keeps the eyes moving across the photo. Try posing one hand slightly higher than the other, or have one hand doing something entirely different from its twin. For instance, if one hand is resting on a hip, the other could be adjusting a tie or lightly brushing away from the face. This not only breaks up the monotony but also adds a story element—like they're getting ready for something, or maybe they're in the middle of a thought.

Overcoming Stiffness

Alright, let's tackle the common foe of every photographer—stiffness. Nothing quite disrupts the natural flow of a photo like hands that look like they've been starched. The trick to overcoming this is encouraging movement and fluidity. During your shoot, keep your subjects moving; let them change positions, or gently shift their weight. This movement helps in loosening up those stiff muscles, making the hands more pliable and easy to pose. Another handy tip is to involve the hands continuously, like running them through hair, adjusting clothing, or even gesturing while speaking. These actions help achieve a more relaxed hand and breathe life into the photograph, making it feel like a captured moment rather than a staged pose.

Practical Posing Exercises

Finally, for those who love a bit of hands-on learning, here are some practical posing exercises you can whip out during your shoots. A great one to start with is the 'pass the object' game. Give your subject something small to hold—a flower, a hat, or a book. Ask them to pass it from one hand to the other, slowly and deliberately, while you snap away. This exercise helps find natural hand placements and eases your subject into being more comfortable with their hands moving freely. Another exercise is the 'conversation hands' where you engage your subject in a casual conversation and ask them to express themselves using their hands as they would naturally. This can lead to some candid shots with very naturally posed hands.

By weaving these elements together—embracing the basics, playing with asymmetry, combating stiffness, and engaging in practical exercises—you'll be able to elevate your hand-posing game. Remember, the goal is to mirror the effortless grace that hands can exhibit when they're not trying too hard to be anything but what they are: expressive, essential aspects of our human experience. So keep these tips in your toolkit, and watch as your photos start to reflect the subtle art of natural hand placement, capturing not just images, but stories, emotions, and moments.

Overcoming Awkwardness: Techniques for Relaxed Hands

Ah, the dreaded hand awkwardness. It's like that one guest at a party who doesn't really know anyone and ends up just standing around, occasionally fiddling with a napkin. In photography, awkward hands can similarly make an otherwise great photo feel a bit off. But fear not, for there are ways to help your subjects relax their hands so naturally that they'll forget they even have them. Let's dive into some techniques that can transform those rigid digits into expressive extensions of your subject's personality.

Breathing and Relaxation Techniques

First up, let's talk about the power of a good ol' deep breath. It's not just great for yoga; it can work wonders in calming down a nervous photoshoot subject. Before you start snapping away, take a moment to guide your subject through a few deep breathing exercises. Have them breathe in slowly through the nose, hold for a few seconds, and then exhale through the mouth. This helps reduce overall tension and can specifically relax the hands, which are often the first body parts to betray nerves. Encourage your subject to shake their hands loosely at their sides after a couple of breaths. This helps release any lingering stiffness and gets the blood flowing. Think of it as a mini reset for the hands, getting them photo-ready and feeling more like natural appendages rather than awkward props.

Communication is Key

Next, never underestimate the power of good communication. I'm talking about reassuring, clear, and friendly guidance that helps your subject feel at ease. It's about creating an environment where they feel they can trust you with their image. Use your words to build this trust. Tell them what you're doing and why, especially when it involves their hands. If you need them to move their hand, explain why it enhances the shot. For instance, "Could you move your hand up slightly? It'll help frame your face beautifully." This not only makes the subject feel included in the creative process but also helps demystify what can often feel like a confusing array of demands. When subjects understand the 'why,' they're more likely to participate willingly and relax into their roles.

The Power of Distraction

Sometimes the best way to deal with hand awkwardness is to distract from it entirely. Give your subject something to hold or interact with. This could be anything from a coffee cup or a book to a prop that complements the theme of the shoot. When subjects have something to hold, it gives their hands a purpose, which can instantly make the hands look more natural and relaxed. For example, during a casual street-style shoot, handing someone a skateboard or a camera can change their focus from worrying about their hands to interacting with the object, which often results in a more dynamic and engaging photo. The hands become an integral part of the story being told, rather than an awkward element to be managed.

Adjusting the Environment

Finally, consider the shooting environment itself. Sometimes, the setting can contribute to a subject's nervousness. If you're shooting in a studio, make it a cozy and inviting space. Play some soft music, keep the temperature comfortable, and maybe have some comfortable seating available for breaks. If you're outdoors, choose locations that aren't too crowded or noisy, which can add to the stress. A calm environment helps in fostering a relaxed atmosphere where the subject feels safe and more at ease. This tranquility often translates directly to how relaxed their hands appear in photos. Remember, a relaxed subject equals relaxed hands, and that's half the battle won in capturing great portraits.

By integrating these techniques into your photography

sessions, you can effectively minimize hand awkwardness, turning those unsure hands into expressive tools that enhance your portraits. It's all about making the subject feel as comfortable and natural as possible, allowing their true personality to shine through, right down to their fingertips. So, next time you pick up your camera, remember these tips and watch as your photos transform from stiff portraits to vibrant, dynamic expressions of human emotion.

Essential Gear for Capturing the Finest Hand Details

Let's talk gear because, let's face it, even the most skilled photographer's eyes widen at the sight of shiny new equipment. But beyond the shiny allure, the right gear can seriously up your hand photography game, helping you capture every crease, line, and detail that hands have to offer. So, whether you're looking to shoot the rugged, calloused hands of a lifelong carpenter or the delicate hands of a newborn, here's your go-to guide for choosing the equipment that will make those details pop like popcorn at a movie theater.

Choosing the Right Lens

When it comes to lenses, think of them as your best buddies in the quest to nail those intricate hand shots. The lens you choose can make or break the level of detail and overall quality of your hand portraits. For starters, consider a macro lens. Why, you ask? Well, macro lenses allow you to get up close and personal without losing focus, capturing details that would otherwise be mere blurs. Imagine being able to see the unique swirls of a fingerprint or the fine hairs on the back of a hand. That's the magic of a good macro lens. But let's not put all our eggs in one basket. Depending on the context of the shot and how much of the surroundings you want to include, you might opt for a standard 50mm or an 85mm lens. These lenses are fantastic for portrait work because they help keep the hands proportionate to the rest of the body without distorting features, making them a versatile choice for more than just close-ups.

Importance of a Tripod

Now, onto the trusty tripod. Think of it as the reliable friend who's always there to support you—literally. Using a tripod during hand detail shots isn't just about avoiding shaky hands; it's about precision. When you're zoomed in capturing the textures and lines of human hands, even the slightest movement can turn a would-be stunning photo into a blurry disappointment. A tripod stabilizes your camera, ensuring that all the minute details are sharp and clear. Plus, it frees you up to tweak lighting, adjust props, or even guide your model without having to reset your camera position every time. And let's not forget long exposure shots where a tripod becomes indispensable. Whether capturing the grace of a pianist's hands in motion or the dynamic tension in a dancer's gestures, a tripod helps you maintain the sharpness of static elements while beautifully blurring the moving parts.

Utilizing Reflectors and Diffusers

Moving on to reflectors and diffusers, these are the unsung

heroes in the world of photography lighting, especially when shooting outdoors or in harsh lighting conditions. Reflectors bounce light back onto your subject, filling in those unflattering shadows and highlighting the aspects you want to showcase. Imagine you're shooting on a sunny day. The harsh light casts deep shadows over the hand's contours, obscuring details. Here, a reflector can be angled to soften those shadows, ensuring the hand's details are visible and well-defined. Diffusers, on the other hand, are perfect for softening direct light sources, creating a gentle, even light that flatters the hand's natural textures. They're particularly useful in softening the light for close-up shots of hands, where harsh light can create distracting glare and overly stark contrasts.

Macro Photography for Hands

Lastly, let's delve a bit deeper into the realm of macro photography for hands. This isn't just about getting close; it's about revealing a world that's often overlooked. Macro photography allows you to capture the smallest details with such clarity and depth that each photo tells a story of its own. From the roughness of a laborer's hands to the subtle nail art on a fashion model, these details can elevate a simple hand portrait to a compelling narrative piece. But macro photography requires patience and precision. You'll need to pay attention to depth of field, ensuring that the part of the hand you want in focus is crystal clear. Lighting, too, plays a crucial role. You'll often find that softer, diffused light works wonders in macro photography, highlighting details without washing them out.

Incorporating these tools and techniques into your hand

photography isn't just about enhancing visual appeal; it's about respecting the story each hand tells. Hands are as expressive as faces, perhaps even more so because they interact so intimately with the world. By choosing the right lens, stabilizing your shots with a tripod, mastering the use of reflectors and diffusers, and embracing the power of macro photography, you bring these stories to light in the most vivid detail possible. So the next time you set out to capture the beauty of hands, remember that with the right gear and a bit of know-how, you're not just taking pictures; you're preserving the marks of lives lived, the imprints of personal histories, and the subtle dance of human expression, all resting at the fingertips of your subjects.

Lighting Techniques for Emphasizing Hand Gestures

Ah, lighting! It's the secret sauce that can turn your average hand portrait into a storytelling masterpiece. Much like a maestro conducts an orchestra, a photographer uses light to direct the viewer's attention and evoke specific emotions. So, whether you're looking to highlight the rugged textures of a craftsman's hands or create a soft, dreamy mood that makes a bride's hands look ethereal, understanding how to manipulate lighting is key. Let's shine a spotlight on some of the most effective lighting techniques that can help you emphasize hand gestures and elevate the visual impact of your portraits.

Directional Lighting to Enhance Texture

Imagine you're looking at a sculpture in a museum. The way

the light casts shadows across the surface brings out every detail, every contour, making it stand out in sharp relief. That's exactly what directional lighting can do for hand portraits. By positioning your light source at an angle—whether it's a natural light coming from a window or an artificial light like a softbox— you can create shadows and highlights that accentuate the textures of the hands. This method is particularly great for showcasing hands that tell a story, like those of a firefighter, a baker, or an elderly person whose hands may carry years of experience. The key here is to experiment with the angle and intensity of your light source. Try sidelighting to capture the texture of the skin and veins, or backlighting to enhance the contours and edges of the hands. Each position offers a new dimension of detail, inviting the viewer to look closer and admire the unique stories those hands tell.

Soft Lighting for Mood

Now, while sharp, dramatic lighting is fantastic for highlighting texture, soft lighting is irresistibly enchanting. It's like the visual equivalent of a gentle whisper—it draws you in. Soft lighting uses diffused light to create a gentle, even spread that doesn't overpower the subject. This type of lighting is perfect when you want to convey emotions like tenderness, peace, or intimacy. Imagine a mother, cradling her newborn; her hands delicately supporting the baby. Soft lighting can wrap this scene in a warm glow, making the viewer feel the warmth and love emanating from the image. To achieve this, you can use diffusers on your lights, shoot during the golden hours of sunrise or sunset, or even use a white curtain to soften the harsh midday sun. The softer the light, the more ethereal and inviting the hands in your portrait will appear, enhancing the emotional resonance of the gesture.

High Contrast Lighting for Drama

If soft lighting is a gentle whisper, high contrast lighting is the bold shout that grabs your attention. It's all about playing with deep shadows and bright highlights to create a dramatic effect that can be incredibly powerful. This type of lighting is ideal when you want to focus intensely on a hand gesture, making it the undisputed focal point of your portrait. For instance, consider a dancer's hands, captured in a moment of explosive motion. High contrast lighting can amplify this dynamic, capturing the play of light and shadow across the muscles and bones, enhancing the drama and intensity of the movement. To create this look, you'll want to use a strong, direct light source and position it in a way that maximizes the contrast between light and dark areas. This technique not only draws the viewer's eye directly to the hands but also adds a layer of theatricality and excitement to your photos.

Playing with Shadows

Speaking of drama, let's not forget the artistic potential of shadows. Shadows are not just absence of light; they're an entity of their own, capable of adding depth, mystery, and intrigue to your photographs. By allowing hands to cast shadows over themselves or other surfaces, you create a layered image that invites the viewer to delve deeper into the picture. Take, for example, a shot where the fingers are spread wide, casting a web of shadows that play across the subject's face or body. This not only highlights the gesture but also adds a visual complexity to the image, making it more engaging and thought-provoking. You can experiment with the direction and softness of the shadows by adjusting the light source and using objects to shape or block the light, creating an endless variety of shadow effects that can transform a simple hand portrait into a narrative-rich masterpiece.

Each of these lighting techniques offers a unique toolset for emphasizing hand gestures in your photography, transforming what could be a simple shot into a deeply expressive, visually arresting portrait. By mastering these techniques, you equip yourself with the ability to not only capture images but to tell stories, evoke emotions, and reveal the profound beauty and complexity of human hands. Remember, light is not just a component of photography; it's the very essence that gives life to your images, so wield it wisely, experiment boldly, and watch as your portraits of hands become works of art that speak volumes.

Cultivating Your Eye: Analyzing Hand Poses in Iconic Portraits

The iconic portraits that have stood the test of time, where every gesture and every detail seems to hold a world of stories. Ever wonder what makes these images tick? A big part of their magic lies in how hands are posed. Hands can push a narrative forward or pull us into the depths of a character's soul without a single word. So, let's roll up our sleeves and dig into the art of studying these masterpieces to elevate our own photographic storytelling.

Studying the Masters

Think of each iconic photograph or painting you admire as a personal tutor in the art of composition and emotional resonance. These aren't just pretty pictures; they are rich textbooks filled with lessons on balancing a frame or evoking feelings with a mere flick of a wrist. Take, for example, the haunting beauty of Dorothea Lange's "Migrant Mother." The way the subject's hands frame her face draws attention not just to her weary expression but also to the strength and resilience conveyed by her grip. Here's a fun exercise: pick out a famous portrait each week and analyze the hand poses. Look at how they contribute to the overall composition and what they say about the subject. It's like detective work, but instead of solving crimes, you uncover the secrets of powerful imagery.

Decoding the Narrative

Now, let's play a bit of narrative detective. Each hand gesture in a portrait tells part of a story. It's up to you, the photographer, to piece these clues together. Consider the subtle details: the direction a hand is pointing, the objects they're holding, the way fingers are spread or clasped. Each element is a piece of the narrative puzzle. For instance, in Yousuf Karsh's portrait of Winston Churchill, the prime minister's bulldog-like determination is echoed in his firm, almost defiant grip on his cane. This isn't just a man standing for a photo; this is a leader unyielding in the face of adversity. When you start to decode the gestures in this way, you begin to see beyond the surface and can start weaving similar depth into your own work.

The Evolution of Hand Posing

Understanding the evolution of hand posing can also give you insights into broader societal changes. Over the years, the portrayal of hands in art and photography has shifted, mirroring changes in social attitudes, aesthetics, and photographic technology. For example, Victorian portraits often featured very formal, stiff poses which reflected the social norms of the era. Contrast this with the relaxed, candid styles of modern-day portraiture that suggest a more open and fluid societal structure. Observing these trends not only helps in understanding the historical context behind certain posing styles but also in predicting where contemporary hand posing might be headed. So, keep an eye on current trends, but also look back to see how past trends evolved over time. It might just give you a clue about what's coming next.

Creating Your Signature Style

Finally, all this studying and decoding should culminate in one thing: forging your unique style. This isn't about copying what's been done but rather taking what you've learned and mixing it with your personal creativity and flair. Maybe you're drawn to the dramatic interplay of light and shadow, or perhaps it's the subtle storytelling of soft, unobtrusive hand gestures that captivate you. Whatever it is, blend these elements with your personal vision. Experiment with angles, lighting, and contexts, and see how different hand poses can change the mood or meaning of a photograph. Remember, the goal isn't to replicate the masters but to use their genius as a springboard to discover and refine your unique photographic voice.

By continually studying, decoding, observing, and experimenting, you're not just taking photos; you're crafting visual stories that speak, touch, and linger in the mind. And isn't that the kind of magic we all aspire to create with our cameras? So the next time you're out shooting, remember these lessons from the past and present, and let them guide your hands (and your subjects' hands) to tell stories only you can tell.

Chapter 2: Creative Hand Poses for Different Photography Styles

Ready to dive into the world of hand posing with a splash of creativity? Think of this chapter as your backstage pass to understanding how hands can dramatically enhance the storytelling in various photography styles. We're about to explore some incredibly artistic and effective ways to position those digits, whether they're adorned in bridal lace or wrapped around a groom's arm. So, grab your camera, flex those fingers, and let's get into the perfect poses that make every shot a story worth telling.

Elegant Hand Poses for Bridal Photography

Grace and Poise

Picture this: It's the big day, and every detail is dripping with elegance, especially the bride, radiant in her gown. Now, imagine her hands awkwardly hanging by her sides like limp noodles. Nope, doesn't quite fit the picture, right? That's where your skills come in. Bridal photography is all about grace and delicacy, and the hands play a starring role. Start by encouraging the bride to soften her hands as if she were about to receive a precious gift. Have her gently touch the fabric of her dress or lightly play with a strand of her hair. Each pose should suggest a natural grace, enhancing not only the elegance of her attire but also the emotional atmosphere of the day. The hands can express anticipation, tenderness, or even reflective tranquility. For an added touch of magic, focus on how the light dances over her fingers, perhaps adorned with a new wedding ring that deserves its spotlight. Soft, side lighting can accentuate the delicacy of her touch and the sparkle of the ring, creating a shot that's as timeless as it is beautiful.

Interaction with Elements

Brides often spend a good amount of time choosing their dress, veil, and bouquet, so let's make sure their hands help showcase these elements. A classic pose you might direct could involve the bride gently lifting a portion of her dress as she moves, giving a glimpse of her shoes or simply adding movement to the static scene. This not only draws attention to the dress's details but also gives a dynamic quality to the image. Similarly, hands adjusting a veil or softly holding a bouquet can convey a narrative of preparation and expectation. Encourage interaction with these elements in a way that feels natural and unforced. For instance, a bride tucking a flower back into her bouquet can capture a candid, spontaneous moment that feels intimate and personal.

Couple's Hands Together

Now, let's bring the groom into the frame. The couple's hands together are powerful symbols of their new union. Look for natural moments where their hands come together, like an intertwined handhold during their vows or a casual but affectionate touch as they walk side by side. These are the moments that often speak louder than words. You might also consider a close-up shot of their hands placed over one another, perhaps on a table or against the bride's dress, highlighting their wedding bands. This kind of shot doesn't just celebrate their individual personalities but also their union, telling a story of partnership and love.

Storytelling through Hands

Every wedding is a unique narrative, and hands can tell a compelling part of that story. Imagine capturing the nervous excitement through a shot of the bride's hands clasping her dress before the walk down the aisle. Or the tender moment when the couple's hands meet, fingers gently entwining, during their first look. These shots do more than document; they evoke emotion and resonance. As a photographer, your challenge is to be observant, to catch these fleeting interactions. Look for the unguarded moments, the spontaneous reactions that unfold naturally. These are the instances where hands help tell a deeper story of the day, one of anticipation, joy, and the myriad emotions that a wedding encompasses.

By focusing on grace, interaction, unity, and narrative, you transform what could be mere snapshots into vivid, emotive moments. Bridal hand poses, when done right, do more than complement the visual aesthetics; they breathe life into the story of the day, making it as enchanting and memorable as every couple deserves. So, keep your eyes open, anticipate the gestures, and let your camera capture the delicate dance of hands that makes wedding photography truly magical.

Dynamic Hand Movements in Dance and Performance Photography

Capturing Motion

When it comes to dance and performance photography, captur- ing the essence of motion is like trying to write poetry with your camera—every movement tells a part of the story, especially the hands. They flutter and flow, or snap and pop, accentuating the dancer's emotional and physical exertions. To really bring out the blur of motion, which beautifully conveys energy and movement, you need to play around with your shutter speed. A slower shutter speed can create that gorgeous motion blur that feels like the dancer is painting strokes in the air with their hands. But here's the kicker, balancing the right amount of blur without losing the sharpness of the dancer can be tricky. It's like seasoning food; too little and it's bland, too much and it's overpowering. Start with a shutter speed of 1/30th of a second and adjust from there based on how fast the performance is. Remember, the key is to capture the flow of movement so vividly that anyone looking at the photo can feel the dance move through them.

Emphasizing the Expressive Power of Hands

Now, while the whole body dances, the hands often tell their own expressive story. They can be soft and supple, or tense and powerful. To capture this spectrum of emotion, zoom in on those hands! Let's say a ballet dancer is performing a delicate routine. Focus on how their fingertips gracefully extend, each finger communicating finesse and precision. Or consider a flamenco dancer, where hands are not just hands; they're an explosion of passion, with every finger snap and wrist flick embodying the intensity of the performance. To really spotlight this expressive power, use a shallower depth of field to bring the hands into sharp focus against a softer background. This technique not only highlights the hand movements but also pulls the viewers' attention directly to the emotions being portrayed through them. It's about making the hands the stars of the show for a moment, letting their motion speak volumes.

Freeze Frame Techniques

Sometimes, though, you want to freeze those dynamic hand movements to capture the peak of a performance's intensity. This is where your shutter speed needs to kick it up a notch. Switching to a faster shutter speed, like 1/1000th of a second, can freeze the action as if time itself has paused, allowing you to capture every detail of the hand's position and the tension in each tendon. It's crucial, especially in fast-paced performances, to not just freeze any moment but to anticipate and capture the 'decisive moment'—that split second where the movement, the emotion, and the story reach their zenith. Good lighting is your best ally here. Ensure there's enough light to avoid unwanted noise or grain in your freeze frames. If you're shooting indoors, don't shy away from bumping up your ISO or using additional lighting to achieve that crisp, clear shot where every droplet of sweat and strand of muscle is gloriously evident.

Interaction with the Audience

Capturing the interaction between the dancers and their audience adds an entirely new layer of depth to your photos. Hands reaching out to the audience or gesturing in a way that involves the viewers can create a connection that feels almost tangible. For instance, picture a scene where a dancer throws their hands out toward the crowd, palms up, as if offering a piece of the performance to the spectators. Capturing these moments requires you to be in tune not just with the performer but also with the audience's reactions. Position yourself in a spot where you can catch both the action and the audience's responses. Sometimes, focusing on the audience's hands, perhaps clapping in rhythm or reaching out towards the performer, can mirror the energy on stage and intensify the communal experience of the performance. This kind of shot not only documents the performance but also the impact it has, telling a fuller story of the event and the shared space between performer and spectator.

By exploring these techniques, you dive deeper into the art of dance and performance photography, going beyond mere documentation to capture the fleeting beauty of motion, the intense expressivity of performers' hands, and the interaction that bridges the gap between stage and seat. So keep these tips in your back pocket, and watch as your dance photography leaps to new heights, capturing not just images but the very essence of movement and emotion.

Capturing Authenticity: Hand Poses for Documentary Photography

The Hands Tell the Story

In the raw, unfiltered world of documentary photography, every wrinkle, every scar, and every bit of dirt captured on the hands of your subjects narrates a tale more gripping than any high-budget drama could hope to portray. Think about the gritty hands of a miner, coal dust settled into their life lines, or the weather-beaten, sun-spotted hands of a farmer, gripping the tools of their trade. These hands don't just do work; they tell the story of a life lived at the coalface—quite literally in some cases. As a documentary photographer, your lens is the scribe that records these tales. When you shoot, consider the historical and personal significance of these hands. Are they the hands of someone who has labored hard for decades, or the delicate, yet surprisingly firm grip of a child in a developing country? Each set of hands holds a narrative waiting to be told, and it's your job to capture this with honesty and respect. When setting up your shot, pay attention to how the light casts shadows in the creases of the hands, how it highlights the callouses and the smoothness or roughness of the skin. These details are your characters, and they are what will pull your audience into the story you're trying to tell.

Contextual Hand Gestures

Beyond the physical appearance of hands, the gestures they make are deeply tied to the daily lives and cultures of your subjects. A gesture as simple as the way a baker kneads dough or the confident, smooth movements of a tailor as they push a needle through fabric are the nuances that bring authenticity to your photographs. These gestures are often overlooked in the hustle of daily life, but in the realm of documentary photography, they are gold. They provide insight into the subject's environment and their interaction with it, offering viewers a glimpse into worlds they might otherwise never know. Capturing these requires you to immerse yourself in the subjects' environments to observe them without interfering. It's about finding the extraordinary in the ordinary, the universal in the specific. For instance, the hands of a potter as they mold clay can speak to the universal act of creation, an act mirrored in every culture and community, though expressed differently across the world's tapestry of lifestyles.

Unposed and Natural

The true essence of documentary photography lies in its ability to preserve moments exactly as they are. Posing your subject or their hands can often strip away the authenticity you're aiming to capture. Instead, let the hands fall where they may, so to speak. Capture the fisherman as he mends his nets, fingers nimbly working with the familiarity of routine; photograph the street vendor as they handle the goods, the exchange of food for money. These hands tell the truth of their lives. Achieving this naturalness requires patience. It's about being a fly on the wall, observing without altering the natural course of your subject's day. It might mean waiting out the perfect shot, being present in the moment, ready to capture the hands as they move naturally, telling their own stories without a script.

Detail in the Mundane

Finally, the true challenge and beauty of documentary photography is in finding the profound in the mundane. Hands flipping a burger at a fast-food joint, a mother's hands gently but firmly washing her young child, an artist's hands covered in paint— they all have stories embedded in their routine. Your lens can elevate these everyday acts into a narrative that resonates with others, finding the connection in human experience that speaks across socio-economic, cultural, and geographical divides. Look for the details that others might miss—the way hands tremble with a barely perceptible nervousness, the strength with which a young girl grips her schoolbooks, the gentle, almost reverent way a gardener handles the plants. These details might seem trivial at first glance, but when captured through your camera, they can turn into powerful images that celebrate the beauty and struggle inherent in everyday life.

In documentary photography, hands are more than just body parts; they are the storytellers and the story, the poets and the poetry. As you hold your camera, remember that you're not just capturing images; you're capturing life, in all its gritty, graceful glory. So let the hands you photograph speak, let them narrate their tales, and let them do so in their most honest, unadorned form.

The Subtlety of Hands in Boudoir Photography

Sensual Not Sexual

In the delicate dance of boudoir photography, guiding hands to express sensuality without tipping into explicit territory is a craft akin to a tightrope walk—thrilling yet requiring impecca- ble balance. You, as the photographer, are the choreographer, and it is imperative to direct with sensitivity and a clear vision. The goal is to create images that whisper rather than shout, leaving much to the imagination while celebrating the human form with elegance. To achieve this, start by fostering a relaxed and respectful atmosphere, setting the tone for a session that prioritizes comfort and trust. When directing poses, encourage your model to think of their hands as tools of expression rather than mere props. A soft curl of the fingers trailing along the collarbone or a gentle resting of the hand along the curve of the hip can convey intimacy and tenderness. It's all about the suggestion of touch, the promise of it, rather than overt display. Techniques such as soft focusing can also help in achieving this effect, where the hands are seen but the finer details are softened, adding to the overall dreamy, ethereal quality of the shot.

Hands as Veils

The art of using hands as veils is a beautiful way to play with exposure and concealment, crafting images that are as intriguing as they are intimate. This technique involves using the hands to partially cover the body or face, thereby controlling what is revealed and what remains a mystery. The hands might shield the eyes, for instance, leaving the viewer to ponder the gaze behind them, or they might be positioned to obscure part of the face, adding a layer of allure and anonymity. The key here is subtlety and intention; every placement of the hand should feel natural and purposeful, not forced or awkward. Experiment with different positions to see how even a slight change in hand placement can alter the mood and message of the image. Lighting plays a crucial role here as well—shadows cast by the hands can sculpt the body in light and dark, adding a dramatic flair to the veiling effect.

Guiding the Viewer's Eye

In any form of visual art, guiding the viewer's eye throughout the composition is crucial, and in boudoir photography, hands can be pivotal in this narrative dance. The placement of hands can effectively draw attention to specific aspects of the portrait, enhancing the storytelling element. For instance, a hand raised to the lips can draw focus to a smile or a thoughtful expression, while hands placed along the lines of the body can highlight form and posture. The photographer's task is to arrange these visual cues in a way that feels both intentional and fluid. Think of the hands as visual punctuation; they can act as commas that invite a pause, or as periods that emphasize a particular point. This control over the viewer's gaze not only enhances the aesthetic composition but also deepens the emotional impact of the image, making the viewing experience both guided and personal.

The Power of Suggestion

Perhaps one of the most captivating aspects of boudoir photography is its ability to suggest rather than explicitly show. Hands are perfect instruments for this, capable of implying more than is visible and firing up the viewer's imagination. A finger pressed against the lips can suggest silence or secrecy, adding a layer of intrigue. Hands tugging at a piece of clothing can hint at undress without showing it, creating a sense of anticipation and movement. This suggestive power of hands adds a dynamic element to the photographs, making them not just images but stories waiting to be unraveled. The beauty lies in the subtleties, in the small gestures that hint at larger narratives. As a photographer, your role is to capture these moments, these suggestions, with a lens that sees not just the body, but the stories the body tells through its every move and every pause.

In boudoir photography, hands are not just part of the body; they are a critical element of expression, capable of conveying sensuality, intimacy, and emotion. By mastering the use of hands in your compositions, you unlock new dimensions in your photography, transforming simple images into rich, evocative narratives that engage, entice, and enchant.

Creative Hands in Fashion Photography: Beyond the Basics

Accentuating the Attire

Let's get real; in fashion photography, clothes are the undeniable stars of the show. But hey, don't underestimate the power of well-posed hands to turn a good shot into a runway-worthy masterpiece. Think of hands as the unsung heroes that bring attention to the intricate details of the attire. For instance, imagine a model in a sleek, long-sleeve gown. Now, if she slightly lifts the edge of her sleeve with a delicately curled finger, it subtly draws the viewer's eyes to the fabric's texture and the sleeve's cut. It's all about using hands to enhance the features of the clothing, like gently pulling on a lapel to show off a blazer's sharp tailoring or softly touching the brim of a hat that deserves a moment in the spotlight.

The magic really happens when hands and accessories come together in perfect harmony. Picture this: a close-up shot where a model uses her hands to adjust a statement necklace; her fingers gracefully frame the jewelry, guiding the viewer's gaze right where you want it. This kind of interaction not only highlights the accessory but also adds a layer of intention and movement to the image, making the fashion pieces more relatable and desirable. So next time you're shooting, think about how hands can serve not just as part of the model's pose but as a guide that points out the very best features of the clothes and accessories. This approach isn't just about creating beautiful images; it's about crafting visuals that make viewers pause and think, "I need that in my wardrobe!"

Breaking the Mold

Now, who says fashion photography has to play by the rules? Let's shake things up a bit. Encouraging models to adopt unconventional hand poses can inject a dose of fresh energy into your work and challenge the norms of traditional fashion spreads. Forget the same old hand-on-hip pose; how about hands that play with shapes or create unexpected silhouettes? Imagine a model's hands pushing against the fabric of a flowing skirt, causing it to billow around her like a cloud, or hands that form angular shapes around the face, adding a geometric flair to a soft, feathery outfit.

Getting creative with hand poses can also mean breaking away from human forms entirely. Ever thought about having a model mimic the gestures of a bird, with hands that flutter and palms that curve like wings? This kind of imaginative posing can transform a fashion shoot into a narrative piece, turning models into characters and outfits into costumes in a visual story. The key here is to collaborate closely with your models and encourage them to experiment and express themselves through their hands. Sometimes, the most striking images come from a spur-of-the-moment idea that breaks all the conventional rules. So go ahead, push those boundaries, and let those hands tell a story that's as unique as your creative vision.

Interaction with Fabric

Speaking of stories, let's talk about the dynamic love affair between hands and fabric, a relationship that can add layers of texture and movement to your photographs. The way a model handles the fabric can communicate a lot about the garment's character. Does she clutch a chunky knit sweater with a firm, enveloping grasp, suggesting warmth and comfort? Or does she let a silky scarf slip through her fingers, highlighting its smoothness and fluid motion? These interactions are visual poetry, my friend.

Incorporate scenes where models pull at their skirts as they turn, or twist a piece of fabric around their fingers. These movements not only draw attention to the material's qualities but also inject a sense of life into the garments. The fabric seems to dance around the model, and suddenly, the clothes are no longer just clothes; they're alive, dynamic. When planning your shoot, consider the type of fabric you want to highlight and how hands can interact with it to showcase its best qualities. Is it the rugged texture of denim or the glossy sheen of satin? Each material requires a different touch, a different type of interaction to really make it pop in your photos.

Creating Shapes and Lines

Let's not forget the artistry in creating shapes and lines with hands that elevate the aesthetic of your fashion imagery. Hands can be incredibly expressive tools that add new dimensions to your compositions. For instance, a model can create a triangular shape with her arms above her head, framing her face and drawing attention upwards, or her hands could trace the lines of a geometric-patterned coat, guiding the eyes along the design.

Teach your models to think of their hands as painters' brushes, capable of drawing lines and shapes that enhance the composi- tion of your shots. This might involve stretching their fingers wide to elongate the lines of a dress or curling them softly to complement the curves of a bodice. It's all about harmony and contrast, about using hands to create visual paths that lead the viewer's eye through the image. This technique not only adds a layer of sophistication to your shots but also makes your fashion photography a form of visual storytelling that captivates and engages. As you explore this dynamic use of hands, watch your fashion stories unfold, one frame at a time, with each hand pose adding a stroke of genius to your artistic narrative.

Incorporating Props with Hands in Still Life Photography

Hands as an Element of Composition

Who said still life has to be still? Throw in a pair of human hands, and suddenly, your still life photography has a heartbeat. Including hands in still life isn't just about adding a splash of humanity; it's about creating a scale and a sense of relatability that pulls the viewer right into the scene. Imagine a classic setup—a vase of vibrant flowers, a draped cloth, and a softly lit backdrop. Now, picture a hand gently reaching in to adjust a flower's position or to trace the texture of the cloth. This simple action does wonders! It introduces a human element that viewers can connect with, making the entire setup feel more alive, more within reach.

Moreover, hands can help establish scale, offering viewers a reference point that helps them understand the size and layout of the elements within your composition. For instance, a hand holding a small, delicate seashell next to a large, rugged piece of driftwood instantly gives viewers a sense of the size disparity between the two objects. This not only aids in comprehension but also enhances the visual story being told, making the image more engaging and understandable. So next time you're arranging your still life, think about how a hand might add a new dimension of life and scale that transforms your composition from a mere arrangement of objects to a scene that viewers can imagine themselves part of.

Telling a Story with Props

Now, let's jazz things up a bit with props. Props are like the secret spices of photography—they can turn a bland setup into a feast for the eyes, especially when combined with hands. Hands interacting with props can convey messages, evoke emotions, and narrate stories without a single word. Picture this: a worn-out writer's desk, scattered with papers and a vintage typewriter. Now, add a pair of hands, one holding a crumpled piece of paper, poised to throw it away, while the other rests on the typewriter, a symbol of frustration and creative block. This scene tells a story, doesn't it? It speaks of struggle, of discarded ideas, and the daunting pursuit of perfection.

Using props effectively requires you to think about what story you want to tell or what emotion you want to evoke. Whether it's a pair of gardening gloves covered in soil to show a love for gardening, or a hand holding a half-eaten apple beside a stack of diet books to comment on the complexities of diet culture, each prop and how it interacts with the hands can set the tone and direction of your narrative. So dig around in that prop box of yours, and don't be afraid to get a little symbolic or cheeky with your choices. After all, every prop in hand is an opportunity to add layers to your photographic story.

Techniques for Holding Props

Of course, how props are held is just as crucial as what props are used. The key here is naturalness and complementing the overall aesthetic. You want the hands to hold props in a way that feels authentic and enhances the visual appeal of the composition. For example, if you're shooting a vintage scene, having your model hold a retro camera loosely by its strap, fingers elegantly curved around the leather, can evoke a sense of casual nostalgia that's both appealing and fitting to the theme.

Teach your models or subjects the art of relaxed hands. Tension in the fingers can translate to stiffness in the photo, which is the last thing you want in a still life that's supposed to feel natural and inviting. Practice different grips and encourage fluidity in the way the hands interact with the props. Sometimes, a slight change in angle or a softer grip can make all the difference in making the setup feel just right. Remember, the hands are not just holding props; they are expressing a relationship with those props, one that should feel as real and as natural as the story you're aiming to convey.

Interaction Between Hands and Props

Finally, let's talk about the dynamic potential when hands and props come together. This interaction is where the magic happens—it's where static objects come to life, fueled by human touch. Imagine a scene where hands are not just placing a letter into an old mailbox but are also lingering on the lid, as if hesitating to let go of the message inside. This adds a layer of emotion, a hint of reluctance, or perhaps hope, transforming the photograph into a scene charged with feeling.

Encourage interactions that go beyond mere placement. Have hands manipulate, adjust, or even play with the props. A hand tilting a picture frame to straighten it, or fingers brushing off dust from an old book's cover, can add a sense of action and care that deepens the emotional impact of the image. These interactions should feel like a dance between the hands and the props, one where each touch tells a part of the story, each movement adds a beat to the narrative rhythm. So next time you're setting up your still life, think about how the hands can dance with your props, not just to create a composition, but to tell a story, evoke a feeling, and captivate the imagination.

Telling Stories with Hands in Street Photography

Candid Moments

Imagine you're wandering through the bustling streets of a vibrant city, camera in hand, eyes peeled for those unguarded, raw moments that only street photography can capture. Now, focus on the hands around you—the way that old man holds his newspaper with slightly trembling fingers, the energetic gesturing of a street vendor, or the tender grip of a young mother holding her child's hand. These are not just hands; they are the silent narrators of the urban tale unfolding before your eyes. Capturing these candid moments requires a blend of patience, timing, and a bit of luck. But when you do it right, oh boy, the stories those hands can tell! They can speak of years of hard work, moments of excitement, or connections between loved ones. The trick is to keep your approach as inconspicuous as possible. Blend into your surroundings, watch, and wait. Often, it's the moments that happen in the blink of an eye that make the most compelling images. Keep your camera ready, your movements subtle, and let the city's hands show you their stories.

Cultural Significance

Now, let's spice things up with a dash of culture. Hands can be powerful symbols, carrying the weight of cultural significance in their palms and fingertips. In street photography, capturing these culturally charged gestures offers a window into the soul of a place. Take, for instance, the vibrant markets of Marrakech, where the handshake that seals a deal might involve a quick, rhythmic clapping of hands, a tradition steeped in local custom. Or consider the serene temples of Kyoto, where hands pressed together in prayer tell a tale of devotion and peace. As a street photographer, your role is to observe these nuances and understand the context behind the gestures. This might mean doing a bit of homework before you hit the streets, or better yet, striking up a conversation with locals to learn about the significance of certain gestures. Remember, every culture has its own language of hands, and cracking that code can add a rich layer of depth to your street photography, transforming a simple photo into a story of cultural identity.

Hands in the Urban Landscape

Let's paint a picture here—imagine a cityscape, maybe the graffiti-laden walls of Brooklyn or the neon-lit streets of Tokyo. Now, add hands to that scene. Perhaps they're spray-painting a mural, forming shadows against the backdrop, or framing a sunset that turns the city gold. Hands can interact with the urban landscape in ways that are both subtle and dramatic, creating compositions that draw the eye and ignite the imagination. Your job is to find these interactions and frame them in ways that tell a story. Maybe it's a set of hands playing an instrument against a backdrop of old brick buildings, or a child reaching up to a towering mural, tiny fingers stretched wide. These are the contrasts and interactions that bring a city to life through your lens. So next time you're out on the street, camera in hand, look beyond the faces and the landmarks. Look at the hands and how they dance with the city around them.

The Human Connection

Lastly, but most importantly, hands are the bridge between individuals, the physical manifestation of connection and interaction. In the diverse tapestry of street life, hands can tell stories of love, struggle, friendship, and community. Picture this: two hands, different in size and color, clasped together over a meal in a crowded food market or the energetic high-five of street performers celebrating a successful act. These moments, captured through your lens, can resonate universally, reminding us of the shared human experience that connects us all despite our diverse backgrounds. Capturing these interactions with authenticity requires you to be both present and perceptive, ready to notice the moments of connection that might pass unnoticed by a casual observer. It's about finding the universal in the specific, the timeless in the fleeting. And in the world of street photography, it's these moments of connection, these handshakes, high-fives, and hugs, that weave the human story into the urban landscape, making every shot not just a photograph, but a page in the larger story of life.

Posing Hands for Powerful Editorial Portraits

Conveying a Message

In the realm of editorial photography, every element within the frame is a deliberate choice, especially the hands, which can be as expressive as a well-delivered monologue. Think of hands as your silent yet eloquent orators, capable of conveying the core message of your editorial piece. For instance, a clenched fist can denote defiance or solidarity, resonating in political or social justice editorials. Conversely, an open, upward-facing palm can symbolize peace, offering, or vulnerability, perfect for pieces that aim to connect on a humanistic level. When setting up your shot, consider what you want the audience to feel or understand at first glance. The positioning, the action, and even the tension in the hands should align with this message. It's like they're whispering the subtext to your viewers, making the communication subtle yet unmistakably powerful.

Adding Depth to the Story

Beyond mere messaging, hands add layers of depth and context that enrich the narrative woven through your editorial imagery. They can tell stories of age, lifestyle, and even social or cultural backgrounds. Imagine a close-up of a seasoned gardener's hands, soil-etched and weather-worn, juxtaposed against the vibrant, tender blooms they nurture. This contrast not only deepens the visual appeal but also enhances the story of renewal and perseverance. In editorial photography, every detail in the hand—from the scars, the jewelry, to the way fingernails are manicured—can serve as visual clues that contribute to the story's setting and character development. These elements provide a backstory without needing a single word, pulling the viewer deeper into the narrative world you've captured.

Creative Constraints

Now, let's talk about creativity within bounds. Editorial themes can sometimes seem like constraints, but here's where you can turn limitations into creative gold. Hands can be posed to complement the theme, enhancing the editorial's message while adhering to its constraints. Suppose your theme revolves around modern technology's impact on human interactions. In that case, you could depict hands interacting with various devices, or perhaps show a stark contrast by having hands engage in traditional board games or old-school craftsmanship. The idea is to use hands creatively to reinforce the theme, making the message clearer and more impactful. Play around with the context—have hands tearing up a tech magazine, or gently cradling an old transistor radio. Each pose should feel like a piece of a puzzle that, when viewers step back, reveals the bigger picture your editorial aims to showcase.

Power and Vulnerability

Lastly, the dynamic dualities of power and vulnerability can be beautifully expressed through hands. This expression is nuanced and requires a keen sense of balance and emotion. For portraits aiming to evoke power, hands can be firm, directive, perhaps placed assertively on a table, or confidently on the hips. These poses exude control and command, resonating with strength and decisiveness. On the flip side, vulnerability can be captured through more reserved, gentle hand poses— like hands loosely clasped together or softly touching a face. These gestures can evoke a sense of openness, honesty, or introspection, inviting the viewer to a moment of emotional intimacy. By alternating between these expressions, or even blending them, you create a complex, richly human portrayal that engages and challenges the viewer, making your editorial portraits not just seen but felt.

In the dance of editorial photography, hands are not just appendages; they are powerful instruments of expression, capable of elevating your narrative and deepening the emotional connection with your audience. Through careful consideration and creative positioning, hands can transform a simple photo into a compelling story, rich with meaning and ripe with intention. So next time you're framing up for that impactful editorial shot, remember, the hands have as much to say as the eyes or the mouth. Listen to them, guide them, and watch your narrative unfold with a newfound depth that only these silent storytellers can provide.

Chapter 3: Addressing Common Pain Points and Questions

Welcome to the troubleshooting hub of hand posing! Here, we're going to tackle some of the most head-scratching, brow- furrowing issues that pop up when you're trying to make those hands look like they belong in the shot rather than awkwardly photo-bombing it. Whether your subjects' hands resemble stiff branches or they just can't seem to relax, this chapter is your go-to guide for turning those woes into wins. So, let's roll up our sleeves (which might be a bit redundant if you're a photographer who wears vests, but bear with me) and dive into the nitty-gritty of solving these common hand posing puzzles.

Why Do My Subject's Hands Always Look Stiff?

Understanding the Cause

Picture this: you're at a shoot, and everything looks perfect.

The lighting is just right, the backdrop is out of a dream, but then you notice your subject's hands—they're about as relaxed as a cat in a room full of rocking chairs. Stiff hands are often the dead giveaway of a subject's nervousness or uncertainty. It's like their hands are trying to make a run for it while the rest of them is gamely trying to pose. This stiffness can kill the vibe of what might otherwise be a great shot. The root of this issue usually boils down to psychological discomfort. The hands are the subconscious mind's favorite tool for expressing internal states, and when a subject is feeling like a deer in headlights, their hands usually stiffen up, ready for flight rather than a photo.

Relaxation Techniques

Now, how do you transform these rigid branches back into expressive hands? Start with some relaxation techniques. Deep breathing is a fantastic start. Encourage your subject to take a few deep breaths—inhale through the nose, hold for a moment, and exhale slowly through the mouth. This not only helps in lowering their overall anxiety but can also loosen up the hands. Post-breathing, a good old shake-out of the hands can work wonders. Think of it like resetting a computer; sometimes, a good reboot is all you need to get things running smoothly again.

Engagement Through Activity

Another great trick is to get those hands busy. Giving your subject something to hold—a prop, a cup of coffee, or even a beloved book — can provide their hands with a purpose, making them look more natural. This tactic is particularly effective because it shifts the subject's focus from the stress of posing to the simple task of holding something. It's a bit like giving a fidgety person a stress ball—it channels the nervous energy in a way that doesn't involve stiffening up like a board.

Continuous Movement

Last but definitely not least, encourage continuous movement. This can be a game-changer in reducing stiffness. Direct your subjects to move their hands slowly—perhaps adjusting clothing, tucking hair behind an ear, or even gesturing as they talk. Movement keeps the hands from locking up and helps in capturing more dynamic, natural-looking shots. It's a bit like capturing wildlife; you want to catch them in motion, in their element, doing their thing. This approach not only alleviates stiffness but also adds an element of candid authenticity to your shots, making for a lively, engaging portrait rather than a static, posed one.

By tackling the root psychological causes with these practical, easy-to-implement strategies, you can turn stiff, awkward hands into expressive, natural parts of your stunning portraits. Remember, the key lies in making your subjects feel as comfortable and relaxed as possible—their hands will follow suit. So keep these tips up your sleeve, and watch those stiff hands relax into beautiful complements to your photographic compositions.

Balancing Focus: Hands vs. Face

Imagine you're crafting a portrait where every element sings in harmony, but there's a tricky duet between the hands and the face—how do you make sure each gets its moment to shine without stepping on the other's toes? This is where understanding visual hierarchy steps into the spotlight. It's like being a director in a play, deciding who takes center stage and when. In photography, especially when hands and faces are involved, prioritizing the subject's face while using hands to support the overall expression is crucial. This isn't just about focusing on the face; it's about making sure the hands don't steal the show unless, of course, that's your creative intention.

Let's talk about the magic of soft focus techniques, a real game changer in managing the focus dance. By employing a shallower depth of field, you can keep those beautifully expressive hands in the frame without letting them overpower the face. It's like having a spotlight that subtly dims on the hands while keeping the face lit up. The technical side of this involves playing with aperture settings; a wider aperture (a lower f-number) throws more of the background (and potentially foreground) out of focus, allowing the face to remain the star of the show. What you end up with is a portrait where the hands add a whisper of support, enhancing the story told by the face without yelling over it.

Now, onto the art of compositional balance. This is where you, as the photographer, need to be a bit of a tightrope walker, finding the perfect equilibrium that allows hands and face to coexist beautifully within the frame. Think about how the hands can frame the face, perhaps gently cradling it or resting lightly below the chin. Or consider the angle of the shot, which can dramatically shift the focus. A slight tilt, a shift in perspective— these can make all the difference in how the hands and face are perceived in terms of visual weight and interest. It's about creating a composition where the hands serve as an elegant complement to the face, each enhancing the other without causing visual clutter or confusion.

Lighting, oh sweet lighting, how it can make or break your focus! Using lighting to guide the viewer's eyes from hands to face or vice versa is like having a subtle, visual nudge that says, "Hey, look here!" Side lighting can dramatically emphasize texture and shape, which is great if you want to highlight the hands for a moment. But when you want to bring the focus back to the face, consider softer, more frontal lighting that evens out features and softens harsh shadows cast by the hands. This doesn't mean your lighting has to be flat or boring; play with nuances. A little shadow here, a soft highlight there—these can direct attention subtly but effectively, guiding your viewer through the portrait like a visual story, from the expressive hands to the emotive face.

By mastering these techniques, you turn every portrait into a carefully orchestrated symphony, where the hands and face each play their parts in perfect harmony. Whether it's through depth of field, thoughtful composition, or nuanced lighting, the balance you create not only enhances the individual beauty of hands and face but also elevates the entire portrait, making it a compelling piece that invites viewers to look deeper and admire longer.

Quick Fixes for Unnatural Hand Poses

So, you're in the middle of a shoot, and despite your best efforts, your subject's hands still look about as natural as a squirrel in a suit. Don't panic! Let's roll up our sleeves and tackle some on-the-fly adjustments that can transform those awkward hand poses into something that looks and feels a whole lot more comfortable. It's all about being quick and effective, ensuring your subject doesn't lose their vibe and the shoot stays on track. Ready? Let's smooth out those hand-posing bumps with some practical, easy-to-apply fixes.

Adjustment on the Go

First and foremost, let's talk about making quick, on-the-spot adjustments. Sometimes, it takes a small tweak to turn a stiff pose into a relaxed one. Start by observing the overall posture of your subject; often, the position of the hands reflects their overall body tension. A relaxed body usually leads to relaxed hands. If you spot a case of stiff hands, gently ask your subject to drop their arms to their sides and shake them out. Then, have them slowly reposition their hands, finding a more natural placement. Sometimes, simply changing the angle of the elbow or the direction the fingers are pointing can make a difference. Encourage slight movements, like a soft bend in the fingers or a gentle resting of the hand on a nearby object, which can help the hands look more purposeful and less posed.

Another great trick is to use the environment to your advantage. If you're shooting outdoors, find a natural spot for the subject to rest their hands, like a tree trunk or a fence. Indoors, use backdrops like tables or chair backs. These props not only provide a place to rest hands but also help integrate your subject more naturally into the setting. The key here is to keep it casual and prompt spontaneous interaction with the surroundings, which in turn, helps relax the hands and makes everything look a lot more natural.

Reference Images

Now, let's say you're finding it challenging to explain the kind of hand pose you're after. This is where having a set of reference images can be a lifesaver. Before your shoot, prepare a collection of photos that showcase a variety of natural hand poses. Keep these images handy on a tablet or even printed out in a binder. When you hit a hand-posing roadblock, whip out these references and show your subject exactly what you're aiming for. This visual aid can make a huge difference in communication, helping clear up any confusion and providing a clear example to emulate. It's a bit like having a map when you're lost; sometimes, you need to see the path to follow it correctly.

Mirror Technique

Here's a fun idea: use a mirror. It's simple but surprisingly effective. Position a large mirror where your subject can see themselves, and let them adjust their own hand poses while looking at their reflection. This method is fantastic because it gives your subject a degree of autonomy over their pose, and they can immediately see what looks good and what feels comfortable. It's a bit like tweaking your posture when you glimpse yourself in a shop window. The instant feedback loop created by the mirror helps subjects self-correct in real-time, often leading to more natural and personally satisfying hand positions.

Feedback Loop

Speaking of feedback, establishing a positive and ongoing feedback loop during your shoot is crucial. This means maintaining open lines of communication with your subject, offering gentle guidance, and positively reinforcing their efforts. Let them know when a pose works well, and be constructive if adjustments are needed. This kind of supportive interaction builds trust and comfort, which naturally helps ease awkwardness in hand posing. It's about creating a collaborative atmosphere where both photographer and subject are working together to find the best pose. Think of it as a dance, where both partners need to be in sync for the performance to shine. By fostering this collaborative environment, you not only enhance the comfort and confidence of your subject but also increase the chances of capturing those perfect, natural-looking hand poses.

Incorporating these quick fixes into your shooting routine can dramatically improve the naturalness of hand poses, turning potential photo flops into fabulous shots. By adjusting on the go, using reference images, applying the mirror technique, and fostering a positive feedback loop, you equip yourself with a toolkit that can handle just about any hand-posing hiccup. So, keep these strategies up your sleeve, and watch as those once- awkward hands start to look like they belong exactly where they are, beautifully complementing your photographic vision.

Making Subjects Comfortable with Hand Poses

Picture this: you're about to start a photoshoot, and while you're setting up, there's this palpable tension you can almost smell, like burnt toast but less breakfast-y and more panic-y. Your subject is about as relaxed as a long-tailed cat in a room full of rocking chairs. That's where the magic of a pre-shoot consultation comes into play. Think of it as a first date with your subject where awkwardness can be gently nudged aside before the actual shooting starts. Discussing and demonstrating hand poses during this consultation can be incredibly soothing. It's like giving a road map to someone who's about to go on a journey in uncharted territory—it provides comfort, clarity, and a sense of direction. Explain why you're choosing certain poses, show examples from previous shoots, or even use your own hands to demonstrate. This not only breaks the ice but also gradually eases your subject into the idea of being photographed, making them feel more like a collaborator than just the focus of your lens.

Now, let's chat about pose practice. This is like the rehearsal before the big play. Encouraging practice sessions before the actual shoot can significantly boost your subject's comfort with various hand poses. You can make this as fun and lighthearted as possible—maybe turn on some music, crack a few jokes, and let them practice posing in a mirror. It's about creating a no-pressure environment where they can see what looks best and feel more in control of their body. This practice not only helps in refining their poses but also builds their confidence. By the time you're ready to shoot, they'll feel more like a seasoned pro than a nervous newbie. Plus, they'll have a better understanding of how minor adjustments can change the vibe of the pose, making them more likely to experiment with their hand placement naturally during the shoot.

Positive reinforcement is your best friend here. It's like watering a plant; a little encouragement can go a long way in helping someone grow and flourish in front of your camera. Compliment your subject when they nail a pose or when they try something new, even if it's not quite right yet. Focus on the progress, not perfection. This builds a supportive atmosphere and keeps the mood uplifted. Everyone responds well to a bit of praise, and in the context of a photoshoot, it reassures your subject that they're doing well, which in turn, can make them feel more relaxed and willing to push their boundaries. It's about crafting an environment where they feel seen and appreciated, which can dramatically loosen up those stiff hand poses.

Lastly, let's turn our attention to creating a comfortable atmosphere. The environment where you shoot can hugely influence how relaxed your subject feels. This goes beyond just choosing a pretty backdrop. It's about making your shooting space as welcoming and stress-free as possible. If you're indoors, control the temperature so it's not too hot or too cold, offer refreshments, and maybe play some background music to soften the silence that can amplify insecurities. If you're outdoors, consider factors like privacy —shooting in a crowded or overly busy location might make your subject feel like they're on display, which can tighten up those hands again. Choose a quiet, secluded spot if possible, or create a makeshift barrier to give a sense of intimacy. The goal is to make the space feel safe and secure, a place where they can freely express themselves without the fear of judgment or discomfort.

By integrating these strategies into your workflow, you ensure that every subject you shoot feels ready and confident, not just about posing but about expressing themselves in front of your camera. The hands, after all, are just one part of the body but getting them right can set the tone for the authenticity and beauty of the entire portrait. So take the time to consult, practice, reinforce positively, and create a cozy environment. These steps might seem small, but they are mighty in making your photoshoots more successful and your portraits more expressive.

Hand Posing for Individuals Unfamiliar with Modeling

When you're working with folks who aren't exactly seasoned pros in front of the camera, which let's be honest, is quite often, guiding them into natural poses can sometimes feel like trying to explain quantum physics to a cat. They're likely not used to the spotlight and the lens, and their hands might end up looking about as relaxed as a squirrel on its first espresso. Here's where we strip back the complexity and keep things super simple. Because really, simplicity is your best friend when you're dealing with modeling newbies.

Simplifying Instructions

First up, let's tackle the art of simplifying instructions. You know how in some fancy restaurants, the menu descriptions need a translation even though they're in English? Yeah, we don't want that. We want the 'cheeseburger and fries' level of clarity. Keep your posing directions straightforward and avoid photography jargon. Instead of asking your subject to "articulate their digits in a supinated position," you might say, "Just tilt your hands like you're carrying a tray." Use analogies familiar to them or demonstrate the pose yourself. It's about making the directions as relatable and easy to replicate as possible, so they feel more like they're mimicking a natural motion rather than trying to decode a cryptic message.

Hands in Motion

Next, let's get those hands moving. Static poses can be a fast track to stiffness, especially for those not used to posing. So, why not start with something a bit more dynamic? Have your subjects move their hands slowly - maybe fixing their hair, adjusting their clothing, or even pretending to text someone. Movement can help dissipate some of their initial stiffness and makes the whole thing feel a lot more natural. It's like warming up before a workout; it gets the blood flowing and the comfort setting in. Capture them in motion, and you'll find those hands start to look a lot less like they're about to conduct an orchestra and more like they're part of a casual, relaxed body language.

Using Props as Tools

Props are not just great icebreakers but also perfect tools for giving those unsure hands something to do. It could be anything from a coffee cup or sunglasses to a book or a hat. Props act like a psychological safety blanket; they give your subjects a sense of purpose and something to focus on besides the camera. This tactic is particularly useful because it diverts their attention away from the stress of posing. Direct them to interact with the prop in a way that feels natural to them. For instance, if it's a book, they can flip through it casually. This approach not only helps in creating more organic and engaging shots but also makes the whole experience a lot less daunting for the subject.

Role-Playing Scenarios

Finally, consider using role-playing scenarios to help your subjects visualize and embody their poses more naturally. This method is especially effective because it taps into the imagination, allowing them to step out of their nervous self and into a character. Ask them to imagine scenarios where they would naturally use their hands. For example, "Imagine you're pointing out something interesting in the distance to a friend," or "Show me how you'd shield your eyes from the sun on a bright day." These scenarios provide a context, making the hand movements part of a story rather than arbitrary poses. This not only makes the pose easier to adopt but also adds an element of fun to the shoot. It's like playing a part in a mini-drama, where the plot revolves around natural movements and expressions.

Incorporating these strategies can significantly ease the process for those unfamiliar with modeling, making them feel more like they're having a fun time rather than undergoing a rigorous posing session. By simplifying instructions, incorporating movement, using props, and employing role-playing techniques, you create a photography experience that is as enjoyable as it is productive. So next time you find yourself working with a modeling newbie, remember these tips and watch how quickly those awkward, stiff hands transform into expressive, natural elements of your stunning photographs.

Creative Solutions for Group Photos and Hand Placement

Group photos can be like herding cats who've just discovered caffeine—chaotic, unpredictable, and everyone's doing their own thing, especially when it comes to hand placement. But fear not, because with a few strategic moves, you can turn that chaos into a chorus line of well-coordinated elegance. Let's dive into some creative solutions that will help you orchestrate those hands into a cohesive ensemble, ensuring your group shots look like a well-rehearsed ballet instead of a spontaneous flash mob.

Coordinating Hand Poses

Coordinating hand poses in a group setting starts with a vision. What mood or message are you aiming to convey? Once you've nailed that down, it's all about giving clear, simple instructions that everyone can follow. For instance, if you're going for a relaxed vibe, you might suggest that everyone show the palms of their hands slightly or place their hands loosely in their pockets. For a more formal tone, having everyone align their hands uniformly, like on a lapel or a table, can add that touch of synchronicity and class. Think of yourself as a conductor, and each person's hands as an instrument in your orchestra. Your job is to ensure that each 'instrument' plays in harmony with the others, creating a visual symphony that's pleasing to the eye. Sometimes it helps to demonstrate the pose yourself or use one member of the group to show others. Visual cues are incredibly effective and can quickly get everyone on the same page.

Hierarchy of Attention

In any group photo, establishing a hierarchy of attention is crucial. This is where you decide which areas of the photo should draw the most attention and which should complement the main focus. Hand placement plays a vital role here. For instance, if the focus is on someone in the center, you might arrange for the surrounding individuals to have more subdued, less eye-catching hand poses, thus directing the viewer's attention naturally to the center of the group. On the other hand, if you want to highlight two people in a larger group, having them engage in a handshake, high-five, or another interactive hand gesture can effectively draw the viewer's gaze. It's like setting up visual breadcrumbs leading the viewer's eyes to where you want them to go.

Interactions Between Subjects

Now, let's add some spice with interactions between subjects. There's nothing quite like genuine human interaction to breathe life into a photo. Simple gestures like handshakes, high-fives, or even playful shoulder pats can inject dynamism and warmth into your group shots. These interactions not only break up the monotony of posed hands but also tell a story of camaraderie and emotion. For example, in a corporate team photo, a handshake between the CEO and a new team member can signify welcome and integration. In a family portrait, a grandparent with a hand on the shoulder of a grandchild can symbolize support and continuity. Encourage your group to engage naturally with each other, guiding them to express genuine emotions through their hands. This approach not only enhances the aesthetic appeal of your photo but also captures the essence of relationships, making the image more impactful and memorable.

Balancing Individuality and Unity

Finally, the art of balancing individuality and unity in group photos is like mixing the perfect cocktail—too much of one ingredient can throw off the entire concoction. While you want some uniformity in hand posing to maintain a cohesive look, allowing a touch of individuality can add character and interest. Encourage subtle variations in hand placement that reflect each person's personality or role within the group. Perhaps the creative director has a more flamboyant hand gesture, while the CFO has a more reserved pose. These subtle differences can make the photo more engaging and give viewers a sense of who each person is, without disrupting the overall harmony. It's about finding that sweet spot where every hand tells its own story, yet together, they sing the same song.

Mastering these techniques takes practice, but once you do, your group photos will transform from mere snapshots into compelling visual narratives that celebrate both the collective spirit and the uniqueness of each individual. So next time you face a group, remember these strategies, take a deep breath, and confidently conduct your visual symphony. Your camera is your baton, and the world is your orchestra.

Dealing with Awkward Hand Sizes and Shapes

Let's face it, not everyone's hands look like they've walked straight out of a hand model casting call, and that's perfectly okay! In fact, it's more than okay—it's fantastic. Those unique hand sizes and shapes bring character and authenticity to your photos, adding that je ne sais quoi that makes an image truly memorable. So, if you've been scratching your head trying to figure out how to work with hands that might look a bit different, whether they're larger, smaller, or shaped in a way you're not used to, buckle up! We're about to dive into the exciting world of embracing and celebrating these differences.

Embracing Uniqueness

Think of each hand you encounter as a unique piece of art. Like any good art, each has its own quirks and features that can truly enhance your photograph. Say you're working with someone who has particularly large hands. These can be a powerful tool in your visual storytelling arsenal, conveying strength or intensity. Or perhaps you're photographing someone with smaller hands, which can add a delicate or tender quality to the image. The key is to view these traits not as challenges but as opportunities to bring something unique to the table. Encourage your subjects to see the beauty in their uniqueness as well. A little positivity can go a long way in boosting their confidence, which in turn, helps you capture their best selves. Remember, beauty is incredibly diverse, and your photography should celebrate that diversity, not shy away from it.

Strategic Positioning

Now, let's talk strategy—specifically, the strategic positioning of hands in your shots. This is where a little know-how can make a big difference. For instance, playing with angles can dramatically alter how hand sizes and shapes are perceived in a photograph. A hand positioned closer to the camera can appear larger, which might be great for emphasizing detail or creating a sense of depth. Conversely, positioning hands a bit further away from the lens can make them appear smaller, which might be useful if you're aiming for a more subdued effect. It's all about perspective. Also, consider the angle of the hand itself—sometimes a slight tilt or a relaxed curl can make all the difference in how natural and flattering the hand appears. Experiment with different poses and angles, and watch how each change can play up the hand's best features while also contributing to the overall aesthetic of the shot.

Focus on Strengths

Every hand, like every person, has its strengths. Maybe it's the graceful curve of the fingers, the interesting lines of the palm, or even the way the light plays off the skin. Whatever it is, make it a point to focus on these strengths. Use lighting to highlight interesting textures or shadows created by unique hand shapes. Play with focus to draw attention to details that might tell a story, like the worn texture of a craftsman's hands or the elegant length of a pianist's fingers. By focusing on what makes each hand beautiful in its own right, you not only create a more compelling photograph but also help your subject appreciate their own unique beauty. It's a win-win!

Inclusive Posing

Finally, let's champion inclusive posing. This means creating poses that accommodate and celebrate the diverse range of hand characteristics you might encounter. Avoid one-size-fits-all poses; instead, adapt your approach to fit the individual. If someone feels uncomfortable holding a pose that doesn't suit their hand structure, find an alternative that feels more natural to them. This might mean modifying traditional poses or even coming up with something completely new and creative. The goal is to ensure that everyone you photograph feels seen, respected, and beautifully represented. This not only improves the comfort level of your subjects but also enriches your portfolio with a wide array of expressive, authentic hand imagery.

Embracing, strategically positioning, focusing on strengths, and inclusively posing hands of all sizes and shapes not only broadens your photographic skills but also deepens your capacity to tell diverse and engaging stories through your images. So next time you pick up your camera, remember that every hand, with its unique size, shape, and story, has the potential to add something spectacular to your photographs. Celebrate these differences, and let them shine in your work.

Q&A: Your Top Hand Posing Questions Answered

Let's face it, even the most seasoned photographers can sometimes feel like they're trying to solve a Rubik's Cube when it comes to hand posing. You've got questions, and oh boy, do I have answers! This little Q&A session is designed to tackle those head-scratchers that keep you up at night—well, maybe not up all night, but definitely thinking twice about how to position those pesky hands.

Common Concerns

One of the most frequent questions I get is, "How do I make hand poses look more natural?" Great question! The trick is to avoid overthinking it. Yes, you heard me right. Sometimes, you've just got to let it flow. Encourage your subjects to think of their hands as extensions of their expressions. If they're happy, what would their hands be doing? Maybe a light touch to the cheek or a playful hair twirl. If they're somber, perhaps hands folded quietly or a gentle grip on a chair. It's all about context. Here's another hot one: "What if the hands look too dominant in a shot?" Ah, the classic power struggle. To dial down the dominance of hands, try adjusting your shooting angle or use a shallower depth of field to soften the focus on the hands, subtly blending them into the overall composition without losing their essence.

Technical Tips

Moving on to some technical wizardry, let's talk about making those hands pop (or not pop, depending on your artistic vision). Lighting is your best friend here. Want to highlight those hands? Angle your lights to cast interesting shadows and highlights across the hands, enhancing their contours and movements. Dealing with shiny skin that turns hands into reflective beacons? Employ diffusers to soften the light, or position your lights at an angle that minimizes harsh reflections. And here's a nifty trick: use a polarizing filter to reduce glare, which can be especially handy for outdoor shoots.

Creative Inspiration

Now, for a dash of creativity. Ever tried thematic hand posing? It's a blast! Let's say you're doing a winter-themed shoot. Have your subjects wear cozy mittens, holding a steaming cup of cocoa, or making playful gestures like they're throwing a snowball. Seasonal themes make the shoot fun and inspire a range of natural, context-driven hand poses. Or how about integrating elements from the environment? A musician might naturally position their hands as if playing an instrument, even if it's not present in the shot. Use what's uniquely available in your setting to inspire how hands are posed.

Continuous Learning

Lastly, never stop learning. Hand posing isn't something you master overnight. It's a continuous journey of discovery and experimentation. Stay curious and keep experimenting with different styles, techniques, and settings. Watch how others handle hand posing—yes, a bit of healthy Instagram stalking isn't a bad thing. Attend workshops, read photography books, and maybe even practice posing your own hands in front of a mirror to understand the mechanics and aesthetics of different poses. Remember, every shoot is a learning opportunity, so make the most of it and keep evolving your skills.

And there you have it—a little cheat sheet to some of your burning questions about hand posing. Keep these tips and tricks up your sleeve, and who knows? Maybe next time, you'll be the one giving out hand posing advice at parties (because, let's be honest, who doesn't talk about hand posing at parties?).

As we wrap up this chapter, remember the golden rules: stay flexible, keep learning, and always aim to bring out the natural beauty and expression in those hands you're capturing. Whether through technical adjustments, creative experimentation, or simply fostering a better understanding and practice routine, every step you take is a step towards more compelling, expressive photography. Now, let's turn the page and dive deeper into the art of photography in our next adventure. Keep those lenses focused and those hands ready!

Chapter 4: Advanced Techniques and Professional Insights

Welcome to the realm where the real magic happens, the deep dive into the wizardry behind those hand poses that leave viewers spellbound. Think of this as your exclusive backstage pass to the secrets that transform good photographers into great ones, where hands do more than just sit pretty—they tell a story, evoke emotions, and captivate the audience. Ready to up your game and learn the fine art of speaking through hands? Let's roll!

The Secret Language of Hands: Advanced Emotional Cues

Beyond the Basics

Diving into the world of hand posing is akin to learning a new language, but what we're tackling here is more like poetry— the nuanced, subtle gestures that speak volumes. It's not just about telling your model to 'look sad' or 'be happy'; it's about translating those emotions into the language of hands. Imagine a scenario where subtle cues, like a barely noticeable tremble of the fingers or an ever-so-slight tensing of the palm, can depict a spectrum of emotions from anxiety to anticipation. These are the advanced cues that turn a photograph into a story, a moment frozen in time that continues to whisper tales long after the viewer looks away. It's about understanding and capturing the minor shifts in movement and tension that reflect complex emotional states. This level of detail requires not just keen observation but also a deep understanding of how emotions physically manifest in our hands.

Psychological Impact

Now, let's talk a bit with psychology. The way hands are posed can significantly influence the emotional impact of an image on its viewers. For instance, clenched fists often evoke feelings of anger or defiance, while open palms can be seen as welcoming or submissive. But here's where it gets interesting — combining these with other elements like eye contact, body orientation, and facial expressions can either amplify these emotions or create compelling contrasts. A smile paired with tightly clenched hands could suggest a struggle to maintain composure or hidden distress. As a photographer, your role is to orchestrate these elements into a cohesive narrative that engages and moves your audience, making each shot a psychological exploration into the human experience.

Symbolic Gestures

Moving on to the cultural runway, symbolic gestures are like the haute couture of hand posing—specific, culturally loaded, and incredibly impactful. These are gestures that carry specific meanings within various cultural or artistic traditions. For instance, in classical Indian dance, hand gestures known as 'Mudras' are used to tell stories and convey emotions. Each mudra has a specific meaning, contributing to a narrative that is both complex and richly adorned with cultural significance. Incorporating such symbolic gestures into your photography not only adds depth but also respects and celebrates cultural narratives, making your work globally relatable and profoundly expressive. Engaging with these gestures requires research and sensitivity, ensuring that their use is appropriate and respectful, enhancing the storytelling without appropriating cultural elements.

Fine-Tuning Expression

Lastly, let's polish those skills with some fine-tuning tips. Matching the perfect hand pose to the mood or message of your photograph is like finding the right spice for a dish—it has to be just right. Too much or too little can throw off the entire ensemble. This fine-tuning involves adjusting the intensity, angle, and interaction of the hands with other elements in the frame. For instance, a slight curl of the fingers, a gentle placement of the thumb, or the direction in which the hands are pointing can drastically alter the image's emotional tone. Practicing this requires patience and a lot of trial and error, but it's worth the effort. Over time, you'll develop an intuitive sense for how slight modifications can enhance the mood or add a subtle subtext to your photos, making your work not just seen but felt.

Engage deeply with these advanced techniques, and watch as your photographs transform from simple images to complex, emotionally resonant stories. The hands, often overlooked, can become powerful tools in your narrative arsenal, speaking a silent language that echoes in the hearts and minds of your audience. Keep experimenting, keep learning, and most importantly, keep communicating through your art. The more you practice, the more fluent you become in this exquisite language of hands, opening up new dimensions in your photographic storytelling.

Collaborating with Models for Perfect Hand Poses

Dynamic Collaboration

Imagine you're at a photoshoot, and there's this electric buzz in the air—not just from the lights and gear, but from a dynamic collaboration brewing between you and your model. This is where the magic of creating perfect hand poses begins. It's not just about you directing and them following; it's a dance, a back-and-forth dialogue where both of you contribute to the choreography of those hands. Think of it as jazz improvisation; you have a melody in mind, but you need the unique flair of your partner to turn it into a masterpiece. Encourage your model to suggest hand poses that feel natural to them, that tell their story. This exchange doesn't just add authenticity to the pose; it invests them in the shoot, making the expressions more genuine and the hands more expressive. And let's be real, who knows their hands better than the person attached to them? They might come up with an angle or a gesture that you hadn't considered but that captures the essence of the shot perfectly. So, keep that communication flowing, and watch as your collaborative efforts elevate the hand posing game to new heights.

Model's Input

Now, let's dial in on the model's input. Have you ever noticed how a shoot changes for the better when the model feels like they're part of the creative process, not just a prop? When models contribute their ideas, especially about hand posing, it not only enhances their comfort level but also brings a slice of their personality into the frame. This input is gold—it's raw, it's genuine, and it's uniquely theirs. Whether it's a subtle way of folding their fingers they picked up as a child or an expressive hand gesture they saw in a vintage film, these personal touches make the images stand out. So next time you're setting up a shot, ask them how they would naturally position their hands if they were conveying a particular emotion or telling a story. This approach not only makes the models feel valued but also brings a richness to the photographs that is hard to replicate with direction alone.

Building Rapport

Building rapport with your models is like brewing a good cup of coffee—it takes time, attention, and a bit of finesse to get it just right. Start the shoot with a conversation, not about the project, but about something they love. Getting them talking and laughing eases tension, which softens their hands from stiff props to expressive tools. Remember, comfort breeds confidence, and confidence can be seen right down to the fingertips. Use their interests and experiences as a bridge to more natural poses. If they play the piano, talk about that and use it to guide how they might naturally position their hands. This not only makes them more relaxed but also infuses a part of their soul into the shoot, making the images more personal and powerful. It's about creating a connection that helps them feel safe to experiment and express, turning good shots into great ones with hands that tell a story as much as faces do.

Real-Time Feedback

Lastly, real-time feedback can turn a good photoshoot into a great one. It's like having a live edit feature where you can tweak and adjust on the go. When you show the model the shots as you work, it boosts their morale and helps them better understand what works and what doesn't. This immediate loop of feedback is invaluable. It allows models to adjust their poses in real-time, experimenting with their hand positions as they see what changes make the most impact on the screen. Say a certain twist of the wrist or a gentle curl of the fingers catches the light just right, highlighting the emotion you aim to capture. Point it out, praise it, and watch how such real-time boosts encourage the model to push their boundaries and innovate further with each shutter click. This process is not just about correcting mistakes; it's about encouraging the model to play an active role in the creative process, making the session a dynamic playground of ideas where each shot gets better than the last.

Navigating through these strategies transforms the traditional dynamic of photographer and model into a partnership, where both are equally invested in the creative output. It's a dance of ideas and expressions, with hands telling as much of the story as the rest of the pose. So embrace these collaborative techniques, and watch as each session turns into an opportunity for mutual creativity, bringing out the best in both your work and your subjects.

From Good to Great: Refining Hand Poses in Post-Production

Subtle Adjustments

You've wrapped up your shoot, and while flipping through the images, you spot a few where the hands could use a little digital magic. Welcome to the world of post-production, where tiny tweaks can lead to major transformations. Let's start with the subtle art of adjusting hand poses without giving your photos that 'overcooked' Photoshop look. Sometimes, all a hand needs is a slight rotation or a minor adjustment in the angle to change the energy of the entire pose. Using tools like the Liquify filter in Photoshop can be your secret weapon here. But remember, with great power comes great responsibility. A nudge here and a tuck there can perfect a pose, but overdoing it can warp your model into territory that defies anatomy and believability.

Another subtle yet powerful technique is adjusting the shadows and highlights on the hands to either draw more attention to them or let them blend a bit more into the background. For example, enhancing the highlights on the knuckles and fingers can make a hand look more active and expressive, adding depth to the emotions you're trying to convey. Conversely, softening the shadows can reduce the weight of the hands in the composition, preventing them from overpowering the face or the main subject of your photo. This dance of shadows and highlights not only enhances the realism of the hand poses but also integrates them seamlessly into the overall mood of the image. Think of it as tuning an instrument to ensure it plays in harmony with the orchestra, not over it.

Highlighting Details

Now, let's shift our focus to those details that make each hand unique—the lines, the textures, the contours. Highlighting these details can elevate a portrait from straightforward to striking. This is where your skills with sharpening tools and clarity sliders come into play. Applying a touch of sharpening to the fingertips, nails, or the textures of the skin can make these details pop, bringing the viewer's attention to the subtle ways in which the hands contribute to the story of the image.

However, it's not just about making these details more visible; it's about using them to enhance the narrative of your photo. For instance, the roughness of a carpenter's hands tells a story of craftsmanship and toil, while the soft, gentle hands of a ballerina speak to a life of grace and precision. By adjusting the clarity to emphasize these textures, you help tell these stories more compellingly. Techniques like dodging and burning can be particularly effective here. Lightening the highlights on a scar or deepening the shadows around the wrinkles can add layers of story and character to the hands, transforming them from mere body parts into storytellers in their own right.

Balancing Elements

Achieving balance in your composition is crucial, especially when hands play a key role in the visual story. The goal is to ensure that the hands complement the scene without dominating it unless, of course, the hands are the focal point of your shot. This balancing act can be managed through selective blurring and the careful placement of focus. For example, if the hands are meant to support the emotional expression but not take center stage, you might opt to soften their focus slightly. This can be done by using a shallow depth of field in shooting or applying a slight blur in post-production.

Conversely, if the hands hold significant symbolic weight in the image, ensuring they are sharply in focus while perhaps subtly blurring other less critical elements can keep the viewer's eyes anchored where you want them. Color grading also plays a pivotal role here; harmonizing the colors of the hands with the overall color palette of the image can create a cohesive look that feels balanced and pleasing to the eye. It's about making sure every element in your frame, hands included, sings in the same visual choir, creating a harmonious and impactful image.

Advanced Retouching

Finally, let's dive into some advanced retouching techniques that can take your hand poses to the next level. Smoothing, shaping, and toning adjustments can be particularly useful. For instance, if you're working on a beauty shot where the hands need to look as flawless as the face, subtle skin smoothing can be applied. This should be done conservatively; you want to maintain the natural skin texture to avoid a plastic, unrealistic look. Shaping can also be a handy tool—perhaps minimally adjusting the contour of the fingers to create a more graceful line or correcting any awkward bends that occurred during shooting.

Toning is another area where you can really refine the look of the hands. Adjusting the temperature of the skin tones to match or complement the face or the body can prevent the hands from looking disconnected from the rest of the image. This is particularly important in fashion or beauty photography, where the harmony of skin tones across the image is crucial for a polished final product. Techniques like selective color correction can help you achieve this harmony, ensuring that the hands not only look natural but also belong to the same world as the rest of the image.

Embracing these post-production techniques allows you to fine-tune your images to perfection, ensuring that the hands in your shots are not just seen but felt, adding depth and detail that elevate your photographic work from good to great. With each adjustment, you're not just editing an image; you're crafting a visual symphony where every element, hands included, plays its part beautifully.

The Power of Shadow and Light in Hand Photography

Dramatic Contrasts

When it comes to photography, playing with shadows and light isn't just about getting the exposure right—it's about using these elements to sculpt your images into something that jumps off the page, or screen, and grabs the viewer by the eyeballs. Now, imagine you're focusing on hands, those complex landscapes of lines and curves on the ends of our arms. By manipulating shadows and light, you can transform these everyday appendages into dramatic expressions of form and emotion. Picture this: a hand with light falling across it in such a way that each crease and crevice is thrown into sharp relief, creating a landscape of peaks and valleys, light and dark. This isn't just a hand anymore; it's a story of life's work, of battles fought and won, of tenderness and toil. The trick here is to position your light sources strategically— sometimes even small adjustments can change the drama of your composition substantially. Experiment with sidelighting to enhance the textures of the skin, or backlighting to create a mysterious silhouette that invites the viewer to lean in closer. Each shadow and highlight tells a part of the story, so think of yourself as a director setting the stage for a play where every shadow counts.

Creating Mood

Lighting setups do more than illuminate; they set the tone and mood of your photographs. With hands as your subject, the way you light your shot can turn a simple pose into a powerful expression of emotion. Soft, diffused lighting can wrap hands in a gentle glow, suggesting warmth and safety, making it perfect for intimate or comforting scenes. Imagine a scene where a parent holds a newborn's tiny hand, the soft light suggesting a cocoon of parental love and protection. On the flip side, stark, harsh lighting can create shadows that add a touch of drama or tension, ideal for more dynamic or charged scenes. Think of a clenched fist on a table, the hard light casting deep shadows accentuating the tension in the knuckles. By adjusting your lighting setup to match the emotion you want to convey, you transform the hands from mere physical forms into carriers of mood and atmosphere, turning them into powerful tools for storytelling in your photography.

Shadow Play

Now, let's get playful with shadows! Shadows cast by hands aren't just byproducts of light; they're opportunities for creativity and storytelling. They can be mysterious, playful, or even slightly eerie, adding layers of meaning to your images. Consider using the shadows cast by hands to create interaction in your compositions. For example, a shadow of a hand reaching towards another object or person in the frame can add a sense of movement or interaction that isn't physically there but is visually implied. This can be particularly effective in telling stories of connection, longing, or even threat, depending on how you angle and position the hands and lighting. Another fun idea is to create scenes where the shadows interact with themselves—a series of hands with their shadows overlapping in a way that plays out a whole narrative on the wall or floor. This not only captivates the viewer but also turns the photograph into a visual puzzle that keeps them engaged, trying to untangle the story you've woven with light and shadow.

Lighting Techniques

To truly master the art of hand photography, you need to become a wizard of lighting techniques. Start by familiarizing yourself with key light and fill light dynamics. The key light is your main light, usually the strongest, and it sets the overall mood of the image. The fill light helps to soften and eliminate unwanted shadows cast by the key light, making sure the details aren't lost in darkness. Manipulating the balance between these can help you highlight the beauty and complexity of hands. For instance, increasing the intensity of the key light while reducing the fill light can sharpen the contrasts and enhance the textures of the hands, making them more expressive. Conversely, using a softer key light with a stronger fill can give the hands a softer, more subtle presence in the image. Also, consider experimenting with colored gels on your lights to add a splash of unexpected color to the shadows and highlights, which can turn a plain image into something extraordinary. These techniques aren't just about lighting a subject; they're about painting with light, with each ray and shadow you cast helping to shape the final masterpiece.

By exploring these advanced techniques, you're not just taking pictures of hands; you're using them to craft visual stories that resonate with emotion and beauty. Through the play of shadow and light, each photograph becomes a canvas where hands tell their own tales, rich with drama, mood, and meaning. So, go ahead, turn on the lights, set the stage, and let those hands do the talking as you capture their stories in the most compelling light possible.

Incorporating Movement and Tension in Hands

Capturing Movement

Let's talk about capturing the dance of digits, where every flick, twist, and snap of the fingers can tell a whole new story. When you're aiming to freeze those fleeting moments where hands are alive with action, your camera settings and your approach need to be sharp—literally and figuratively. First off, crank up that shutter speed. You want to catch those hands mid-gesture, whether they're strumming a guitar, tossing a pizza dough, or simply waving a dramatic goodbye. A fast shutter speed, think 1/500th of a second or quicker, stops the motion so crisply that you can almost feel the air move around those busy hands.

But hey, life isn't always lived at high speed, right? Sometimes, you want to capture the blur, the graceful sweep of a hand moving through space. Here's where you can dial down that shutter speed for a more artistic take. Let those hands paint strokes of motion across your image, creating a trail of movement that adds a layer of dynamism to your shots. This technique works wonders in conveying the energy and the emotion of the moment—like the passionate blur of a conductor's hands at the crescendo of a symphony or the smooth sweep of a painter's arm across a canvas. Remember, the key here is to keep the rest of your subject relatively sharp, so adjust your ISO and aperture accordingly to maintain a good exposure without sacrificing the crispness of the overall image.

Conveying Tension

Now, onto the gripping world of tension. Hands can be powerful storytellers when it comes to depicting strain or stress. It's all in the way you pose them. Clenched fists, white-knuckled grips, fingertips pressing into palm—these are all universal signals of tension that resonate with viewers on a visceral level. But capturing this tension effectively requires more than just telling your model to 'look stressed'. You need to create a context, build a scenario that naturally leads to these expressions. For instance, have your model grip a rope or hang onto the edge of a chair, anything that naturally encourages their hands to tense up. The real trick is in your timing. Snap the shot at the peak of their grip, right when their muscles are tightest and their concentration is palpable. This not only enhances the realism of the tension but also pulls the viewers into the moment, making them almost feel the strain in their own fingers.

Blurring Techniques

Blurring isn't just for those who forgot their glasses. In the art of photography, intentional blurring of hand movement can transform a static image into a whirlwind of emotions. This technique is perfect for capturing actions that are too fast for the eye to see but too beautiful not to immortalize. Think of a chef's hands in a flurry of chopping, or a pianist's fingers flying over the keys. To achieve this, you'll want to play with a slower shutter speed than usual but not too slow — just enough to capture the essence of movement without losing the form entirely. A good starting point might be around 1/30th to 1/60th of a second. And here's a little secret: combine this with a bit of panning, moving your camera along with the motion of the hands, and you'll get a shot that's sharp in all the right places but deliciously blurred in motion. It's like capturing a dance, each movement trailing a ghostly echo of where it's been.

Static vs. Dynamic

In the world of hand poses, there's a time for stillness and a time for motion, and knowing when to use each can set your photos apart. Static hand poses are all about stability and clarity. They're your go-to when you need to showcase detail or when the emotion of the scene is quiet, introspective. Here, every line, every wrinkle, and every nail is a part of the story, and the stillness lets your audience take it all in. But then, there are times when only a dynamic hand pose will do— when you want to capture the chaos of a moment, the raw, unbridled emotion that can only be expressed in motion. These are the poses that feel like they're bursting out of the frame, hands reaching, throwing, or shielding.

Choosing between these two comes down to the story you're telling. Is it a tale of calm and serenity, or one of action and drama? Adjust your technique accordingly, and don't be afraid to mix things up within the same shoot. Sometimes, the contrast between the calm of a static pose and the energy of a dynamic one can make for a compelling narrative, pulling your viewers deeper into the story you're weaving with every shot.

Expert Tips on Directing Non-Professional Models

When you're shooting with folks who haven't spent much time in front of a camera, think of yourself not just as a photographer but as a guide in a wild, slightly bewildering landscape of lenses and lights. Your job? To make that landscape feel like a walk in the park. Let's start with something I like to call 'Photography Speak Lite'. It's like the diet version of your usual photography jargon. Instead of talking about 'high ISO noise levels' or 'shutter speeds', keep it simple. Use everyday language that anyone could understand. Say things like, "I'm going to make the camera take pictures really quickly" instead of "I'm increasing the shutter speed." This approach keeps your instructions clear and free of confusion, helping your models feel more at ease because they actually understand what you're asking of them.

Visual examples are your best friend. Before the shoot, why not pull up a few photos or even use your own hands to show what you mean by phrases like 'soften your fingers' or 'tilt your hand slightly'? It's one thing to tell someone what to do, and quite another to show them. This not only makes it easier for your model to grasp what you're aiming for but also adds a visual element to the learning process, making it more engaging and easier to remember. Think of it as the difference between reading a recipe and watching a cooking show. One clearly gives you a better sense of what you're supposed to be doing.

Encouraging natural movement might sound like you're asking your models to do a spontaneous dance, and well, that's not entirely off the mark. The best photographs often come from moments of genuine, fluid motion rather than stiff, posed ones. Ask your model to walk around a bit, adjust their hair, laugh, or look away from the camera and then back again. These actions can lead to more relaxed and natural-looking hand positions, capturing the essence of the person rather than just their appearance. It's about creating an environment where they can forget the camera is there, letting their guard down and their natural charisma shine through. The trick is to keep them moving, keep them chatting, and keep them engaged. The more they're thinking about the interaction, the less they're worrying about the camera.

Adjusting your expectations is crucial when working with non-professionals. Remember, they might not be able to hold a pose perfectly, and that's okay. What's important is capturing their genuine expressions and making the experience enjoyable for them. If a pose isn't working, switch it up. If they look uncomfortable, take a break. Your flexibility and patience not only make for a better shoot but also teach you to think on your feet and adapt to unexpected situations. Each non-professional model brings their own unique flavor to the shoot, and sometimes, the most unanticipated poses can turn out to be the most compelling. So, keep an open mind, adjust your plans as needed, and cherish the unpredictability—they might just give you some of your best shots.

Navigating a photoshoot with non-professional models doesn't have to feel like directing traffic during a city blackout. With clear, simple guidance, practical visual examples, encouragement of natural movement, and adaptable expectations, you can turn potential chaos into a collection of captivating, authentic photographic moments. Remember, the goal isn't just to capture great pictures but also to ensure a great experience for your models. When they're comfortable and having fun, it shows in every shot, making your job a whole lot easier and a lot more enjoyable. So keep these tips in mind, and watch as your amateur models rise beautifully to the occasion, one naturally posed hand at a time.

Unique Hand Poses for Unconventional Shoots

Breaking the Mold

Ready to shake things up a bit? When it comes to hand posing, stepping off the beaten path can lead to some truly eye-catching shots. It's about daring to be different, tossing the rulebook out the window, and letting your creative instincts take the lead. Think about it—how often have you seen a photo and thought, "Wow, I've never seen hands posed like that before"? That's the kind of reaction you're aiming for. To get there, start by challenging every traditional pose you know. Ask yourself, "What if?" What if you had a model twist their hands in an unusual way, or use their fingers to mimic the legs of a spider crawling up a wall? These kinds of unconventional poses can inject a playful, surreal, or even slightly unsettling element into your photos, making them stand out in a sea of sameness.

Experimenting with non-traditional hand poses also opens up new ways to use hands as symbols in your imagery. For instance, hands clawed into a ball might represent tension or fear, while hands splayed wide against a stark background could symbolize freedom or surrender. The key here is to let your imagination roam wild and free. Use hands to paint a picture, to tell a story without words, to evoke emotions in a way that conventional poses might not. And remember, unexpected doesn't have to mean complicated. Sometimes, the simplest twist on a traditional pose can be the most effective. So, play around, try new things, and watch as your hands start speaking louder than words.

Conceptual Posing

Moving into the realm of conceptual hand posing, we dive deeper into the narrative potential of hands. Here, every pose is packed with purpose, every gesture is heavy with meaning. This approach requires you to think of hand poses not just as physical forms, but as integral elements of your photo's story. For example, imagine you're shooting a series themed around the concept of struggle and breakthrough. Hands breaking through a paper wall could powerfully visualize this theme, turning a simple action into a symbol of overcoming barriers, both literal and metaphorical.

To master conceptual hand posing, start with the story you want to tell or the emotion you want to convey. Sketch out your ideas—literally, if that helps—and think about how hands can act out these themes. It's like assigning roles to an actor, only here, your actors are hands. And just like in theatre, the context can dramatically shift the interpretation of these poses. Hands cupped around a light source can signify discovery or enlightenment, while the same hands around a dark object might suggest secrecy or protection. The beauty of conceptual posing lies in its flexibility and depth, allowing hands to speak volumes, adding layers of meaning that draw viewers deeper into the image.

Artistic Influences

Now, let's talk about drawing inspiration from the wider world of art. The greats—be they painters, sculptors, or performance artists—can teach us a lot about the power of hands. Take a leaf from Michelangelo's book; his sculptures often feature hands that tell as much of a story as the faces or bodies they're attached to. Or consider how contemporary artists use hands in installations or live performances to communicate messages or challenge perceptions.

Bring these influences into your photography. Study artworks where hands play a crucial role, and use these observations to inform your own posing techniques. Perhaps the delicate, almost translucent hands in a Baroque painting inspire you to use light more creatively, casting gentle shadows that hint at fragility or grace. Or maybe the exaggerated, almost grotesque hands in an expressionist piece encourage you to explore more dramatic, impactful posing. Whatever your source of inspiration, the key is to adapt these artistic lessons into your photographic style, using hands to craft a visual language that's both uniquely yours and deeply rooted in the broader spectrum of art history.

Thematic Consistency

Lastly, maintaining thematic consistency is crucial, especially when you're playing around with unconventional poses. It's the glue that holds your shoot together, ensuring that even the most avant-garde hand poses feel integral, not incidental. This means that every chosen hand pose should reinforce the overarching theme or mood of the shoot. If your theme is about elegance and refinement, even the most unusual hand poses should still carry an air of grace; think hands mimicking the flow of water, or gently swirling like smoke. Every pose, no matter how offbeat, should feel like it belongs in the narrative you're weaving.

Achieving this consistency involves planning and foresight. It requires you to think critically about how each element— lighting, setting, costume, and yes, hand posing—contributes to the final image. It's about ensuring cohesion between concept and execution, making sure that every hand pose, no matter how unconventional, serves the story you're telling. This attention to thematic consistency not only enhances the impact of your photos but also ensures that the narrative thread runs clearly and compellingly through your entire series.

Embrace these strategies, and you'll find yourself not just taking photos, but making art. With each shoot, you'll push the boundaries of what hand posing can do, turning every session into an opportunity to explore, experiment, and express in ways that challenge both you and your viewers. So go ahead, break the mold, draw from the arts, dive into concepts, and weave your themes into every shot. The world of hand posing is vast and varied—explore it with curiosity, and craft your images with care.

Professional Photographers Share Their Signature Hand Poses

Signature Styles

Alright, let's pull back the curtain and peek into the studios of some top-notch photographers to see how they make magic with hand poses. Imagine you're flipping through the pages of your favorite photography book, and you come across an image where the hands alone tell you everything you need to know about the subject. That's the power of a signature hand pose. Each photographer develops a unique style, often through years of tweaking and experimenting, until they find that sweet spot where every finger placement speaks volumes. For instance, one might be known for their ability to capture hands in motion—fingers elegantly poised as if they're dancing on air—creating a sense of movement so palpable, you can almost hear the music. Another might specialize in the raw, unadorned truth of hands—wrinkled, rugged, and powerful, telling stories of hard work and the beauty of age. These signature styles aren't just about aesthetics; they're about perspective, about seeing hands as characters in their own right, each with a story to tell. By studying these styles, you can start to understand the thought process behind each pose—why a slight curl of the fingers was chosen over a flat hand, or why hands are framed against a dark background to emphasize texture and form. This insight is invaluable as it opens up a whole new dimension of hand posing that goes beyond the technical to the deeply personal and creative.

Behind the Scenes

Now, let's go behind the scenes—where the real action happens. It's one thing to admire a beautifully posed set of hands in a photograph; it's another to see how it's done. This glimpse into the process can be incredibly enlightening. Picture a busy photo shoot where the photographer is working closely with the model, guiding them on how to relax their hands, how to position them to catch the light just so. It's a dance of communication and adjustment, where the photographer might gently shift a finger, soften a palm, or demonstrate the pose to achieve the desired effect. This interaction is often where the magic happens. It's not just about placing hands; it's about evoking emotion and expression through touch, pressure, and placement. Seeing this process can demystify hand posing and inspire you to be more hands-on (pun intended) in guiding your models. It shows that great posing is not a happy accident—it's the result of careful, thoughtful direction and a deep understanding of how hands can convey emotion and tell stories.

Adapting Techniques

Adaptation is the name of the game here. While it's great to learn from the masters, the real challenge— is in making these techniques your own. This means taking what you've learned from observing other photographers and tweaking it to fit your style and the needs of your subjects. Suppose you're inspired by a photographer who excels in capturing the elegance of hands in fashion photography. You could take this technique and adapt it to more casual, everyday shoots by focusing on the natural grace in the hands of your subjects, perhaps while they're holding a cup of coffee or flipping through a book. The key is to keep the essence of the technique—emphasizing grace and elegance—while making it relatable and suited to the context of your shoot. This adaptation not only broadens your skill set but also makes your work versatile and personal, reflecting not just your influences but also your individual perspective and creative voice.

Innovation and Creativity

Lastly, let this be a springboard for your own creativity. Studying the signature poses of renowned photographers should be a launching pad, not just a lesson. Use these insights as a catalyst to experiment with new ideas, to push the boundaries of what hand posing can be. Maybe you'll develop a signature pose that involves unconventional objects, or perhaps you'll find a way to express complex narratives through simple gestures. The possibilities are as limitless as your imagination. Let these examples inspire you to think outside the box, to see hands not just as parts of a body but as powerful tools of expression, capable of adding depth and emotion to your photographs in ways you've never considered before. Your signature style— one day, it might be your hands that aspiring photographers are trying to emulate.

As we wrap up this chapter, remember that the journey through the world of hand posing is one of constant learning and creative exploration. From the nuanced expressions captured by seasoned professionals to the innovative techniques that challenge our perceptions of what hand posing can be, there's always something new to discover and adapt. So keep experimenting, keep refining, and most importantly, keep sharing your unique vision through the powerful language of hands. Now, let's turn the page and explore new horizons in the next chapter, where we'll dive even deeper into the art and science of photography, uncovering more secrets and developing further skills that will enhance your photographic journey.

Chapter 5: The Impact of Culture and Context on Hand Posing

Ever found yourself in a bustling foreign market, camera in hand, ready to capture the essence of local life, only to pause and wonder if your gesture for a photo might accidentally start an international incident? Well, you're not alone! The world of hand gestures can be a minefield of misunderstandings, but fear not! This chapter is your cultural compass, guiding you through the fascinating landscape of hand gestures across the globe. So, let's jazz up our hand gesture game and dive into the world where a thumbs-up isn't always a good thing!

Understanding Cultural Significance of Hand Gestures

Universal vs. Culture-Specific Gestures

In the grand theater of human communication, hands are like versatile actors, capable of expressing a plethora of emotions and messages. Some hand gestures are the A-listers, universally recognized and adored. The peace sign, a wave goodbye, or a simple handshake—these have made their way into the global lexicon, understood in countless countries without a hitch. But then, there are the indie gestures, those specific to particular cultures that don't quite make the international cut. Consider the 'moutza' in Greece, where an open palm thrust forward can be highly offensive, a far cry from the benign stop gesture you might use to halt traffic while capturing a street scene. This distinction between universal and culture-specific gestures is crucial for photographers. It's like knowing the difference between shooting in automatic or manual—both can get the job done, but understanding the nuances can make or break your shot.

Significance of Hand Gestures

Delving deeper, each hand gesture carries a story, a snippet of the cultural DNA that can be incredibly revealing. For instance, the Italian 'mano a borsa', where the fingers come together as if holding a tiny purse, speaks volumes about the Italian emphasis on questioning and discourse. In contrast, the Japanese gesture of drawing an 'X' across one's arms signals a strong 'no', reflecting the culture's indirect communication style. As photographers, grasping these meanings can transform a simple photo into a narrative masterpiece, adding layers of context that resonate with viewers across borders. It's about turning your lens into a bridge, connecting the viewer to distant cultures through the silent language of hands.

Research and Awareness

Now, here comes the homework part (groan,I know, but stick with me!). Before you set off on your photographic conquests, a little research can go a long way. Understanding the hand gestures of the culture you're visiting is akin to learning the basic phrases in a foreign language. It's about respect, about approaching your subjects not just as scenes to be captured, but as stories to be understood. This research phase is where you equip yourself with the knowledge to navigate the cultural waters smoothly, ensuring your photography is a form of exchange, not intrusion.

Case Studies

Let's lay out some real-life oopsies to illustrate just how dicey things can get. Picture this: a well-meaning photographer gives the thumbs-up to a group of youths in Iran, hoping to break the ice. Little did they know, that gesture is akin to a middle finger in some Middle Eastern countries. Snap! The mood shifts, the smiles falter, and our photographer is left puzzled, thumb still in the air. These are the moments that underscore the power of gestures and the importance of cultural literacy in photography. Each misunderstood gesture teaches us a lesson in humility and the need for cultural sensitivity, turning each click of the shutter into a learning opportunity.

So, as we navigate through this chapter, keep your minds open and your gestures neutral (at least until you've finished this section!). With each page, we'll turn confusion into clarity and photographs into gateways of cultural understanding, one hand gesture at a time. Now, let's continue our exploration and ensure that the only thing your photography captures is the beauty and complexity of human expression, not a cultural faux pas.

The Role of Hands in Cultural and Religious Ceremonies

When you think about the rituals and ceremonies that stitch the fabric of various cultures together, it's not just the pomp and vibrant colors that catch the eye—it's also the subtle language of hands weaving through the air, each movement rich with symbolism. Imagine the intricate mudras in a classical Indian Bharatanatyam dance, where each hand gesture is a word in a visual language that tells ancient stories of gods and goddesses. Or picture the solemn moments in a Christian wedding, where the joining of hands embodies the binding of two lives. These gestures do more than just decorate the ceremony; they are the ceremony, imbued with centuries of tradition and meaning.

Now, let's talk about capturing these moments — because let's face it, snagging an invite to these cultural showcases is a photographer's dream! But here's the kicker: snapping photos isn't just about getting a good angle; it's about respect. Before you even think about clicking the shutter, make sure you've got the green light. Some ceremonies might consider photographs taboo, or there might be specific moments when cameras should be tucked away. And understanding the context? Non-negotiable. It's like knowing why people throw rice at weddings—without the why, it's just a bizarre food fight. Engage with the community, or better yet, find a cultural guide who can walk you through the dos and don'ts.

They can help you understand not just when and what to shoot, but the significance of what's unfolding before your lens.

Let's not forget the gold mine of learning that these ceremonies offer. Every ritual is a chapter of history, every gesture a brush-stroke of culture. As photographers, we're not just capturing images; we're capturing heritage. Take the time to learn the stories behind the gestures. Why do Buddhist monks gesture with one hand raised and one hand lowered during blessings? What does it symbolize when Muslim worshippers raise their hands to their ears during prayer? This isn't idle curiosity—it's the stuff that adds depth to your photos, transforming them from mere snapshots into narratives.

Incorporating these elements into portrait photography can be just as transformative. Imagine a portrait where a young girl's hands are posed in the Anjali Mudra, a gesture of greeting and prayer common in several Asian cultures. Such a pose doesn't just create visual interest; it weaves her cultural identity into the fabric of the portrait. It's about creating images that tell stories, that celebrate heritage, and that respect the rich tapestry of human culture. So next time you're framing a shot, whether it's at a bustling festival or a quiet ritual, remember: the hands are not just part of the picture. They are the picture, echoing centuries of culture in the space of a single gesture.

Hand Posing Etiquette Across Different Cultures

Navigating the delicate dance of cultural etiquette in photography isn't just about snapping stunning visuals; it's about weaving respect and understanding into the fabric of your interactions. Picture this: you're on a bustling street in Tokyo, camera in hand, and you want to capture the elegance of a traditional tea ceremony. Knowing the dos and don'ts of hand gestures can make the difference between a warm welcome and a cold shoulder. So, let's get you dialed into the etiquette of hand posing across cultures, ensuring your photography is as culturally savvy as it is visually compelling.

First up, let's talk guidelines. Just like you wouldn't wear flip-flops to a business meeting (unless it's at a beach resort, then by all means!), certain hand gestures are big no-nos in various cultures. In some places, like parts of Africa and Asia, handing someone something with your left hand might be considered impolite or even dirty. Meanwhile, a thumbs-up, which you might use to signify "great job!" back home, could be offensive in countries like Iran or Greece. The key to mastering this cultural ballet is to do your homework before you even pack your camera. A quick guide or cheat sheet of common hand gestures can save you from accidental gaffes. Better yet, observe the locals and see how they use their hands in communication. When in doubt, a polite, non-committal hand gesture coupled with a smile goes a long way.

Now, let's consider the comfort of your subjects. Imagine you're asking someone to pose for you in a way that's culturally sensitive, like avoiding the use of certain fingers or hand placements that could be seen as rude. By showing that you understand and respect these nuances, you not only make your subjects more comfortable but also open the door to more authentic and relaxed expressions. This respect can transform a stiff, awkward pose into a natural and engaging photograph. It's about creating a space where everyone feels respected and understood, which in turn fosters a better environment for both photography and genuine human connection.

Adjusting your techniques to align with cultural norms doesn't mean stifling your creativity—think of it as a creative challenge! For instance, if you learn that direct eye contact is considered confrontational in a particular culture, you could adjust your approach to focus more on profile shots, or use hand gestures to direct the viewer's attention within the frame. This not only ensures cultural sensitivity but also pushes you to think outside the box and develop new methods that might yield unexpectedly captivating results. It's about finding that sweet spot where respect meets creativity, ensuring your photographs are not just seen, but also felt.

Building trust is the cornerstone of any successful portrait session, especially when crossing cultural lines. When your subjects see that you're making an effort to respect their cultural norms, especially in how they pose their hands, it builds a bridge of trust. This trust is crucial, not just for the few minutes you spend snapping photos, but for the broader goal of cultural exchange and understanding. It turns a simple photo shoot into an opportunity for cross-cultural connection, where each gesture and pose becomes a mutual exploration of values and traditions. And let's be honest, who doesn't want their photography to be more than just pictures, but a passport to cultural bridges and human stories?

So, as you venture into diverse settings with your camera, remember that understanding hand posing etiquette isn't just about avoiding faux pas; it's about embracing the rich tapestry of human culture through your lens. With each respectful gesture and adjusted pose, you're not just capturing images; you're capturing hearts. And in the world of photography, that's the biggest win of all. Let these insights guide you as you continue to explore the fascinating interplay of culture, context, and creativity in the chapters ahead.

Adapting Hand Poses for International Clients

When you're a photographer working with a kaleidoscope of international clients, mastering the art of cross-cultural communication is as crucial as nailing the perfect exposure. It's about more than just speaking the same language or avoiding faux pas; it's about tuning into the subtle frequencies of different cultural expectations and sensitivities. Think of it as being a DJ at a global dance party; you need to know which tunes will get everyone grooving and which ones might clear the dance floor!

Cross-cultural communication in photography isn't just about overcoming language barriers. It's about understanding the unspoken, the gestures, and the cultural nuances that speak volumes. For instance, when you're directing a photoshoot with clients from a culture different from your own, the usual "just act natural" might not cut it. What feels natural in one culture might be awkward or even inappropriate in another. This is where your skills in cross-cultural communication come into play. You start by doing your homework, getting to know the cultural norms and preferences of your clients. Are there specific hand gestures or poses that are favored in their culture? What's considered respectful or beautiful? The answers to these questions can guide how you direct the shoot, ensuring that the poses are not only beautiful but culturally resonant.

Now, let's talk customization. Tailoring hand poses to meet not just the aesthetic preferences but also the cultural expectations of your international clients can turn a good portrait into a great one. This is where you get creative, blending your photographic style with cultural elements. Say you're working with a client from India. Incorporating traditional Indian hand gestures, like the mudras used in classical dance, can add a layer of cultural significance and personalization to the shoot. It shows that you're not just taking a picture; you're telling their story, their way. And it's not just about the big, obvious gestures. Sometimes, the magic is in the details—the slight turn of a wrist or the way fingers are held together can speak volumes about a person's heritage and identity.

Feedback and Adjustment Process

Crafting the perfect hand pose often requires a bit of back and forth, a dance between your vision and your client's comfort. This is where the feedback and adjustment process comes into play. Think of it as sculpting; with each piece of feedback, you refine and adjust, getting closer to the ideal form. Start by showing your clients the poses you have in mind during the pre-shoot consultation. This visual aid can spark discussion, allowing you to gauge their comfort and get their input. Maybe they have ideas on how they could modify a pose to suit their style or cultural background better. During the shoot, keep this dialogue open. Show them the shots as you go, and be ready to tweak and adjust. This collaborative approach not only ensures that the final images meet their expectations but also makes the experience more enjoyable for them. It's about building a partnership, where they feel part of the creative process, not just the subject of it.

Navigating the nuances of hand poses for international clients isn't just about being culturally aware; it's about being culturally engaged. It's about using your camera to bridge gaps, to celebrate diversity, and to tell stories that resonate across cultural divides. With each client, each shoot, you're not just taking photos; you're weaving a global tapestry, rich with the colors and textures of the world's cultures. Keep this guide handy, and watch as your portfolio transforms into a vibrant mosaic of human connections, each hand pose a testament to the beauty of our diverse world.

Expressive Hands in Cultural Portrait Photography

When it comes to portrait photography, nothing quite captures the essence of a person's cultural identity like the expressive power of their hands. Imagine a portrait where a person's hands are sculpted into a traditional Thai greeting or 'wai', where the palms are pressed together in a prayer-like fashion, eloquently conveying a sense of respect and cultural reverence. This gesture alone can speak volumes about the subject's heritage and personal significance, offering a deeply personal glimpse into the cultural tapestry that forms part of their identity. It's these subtle yet powerful expressions that can transform a simple portrait into a narrative piece, telling stories not just through faces, but through the hands that have shaped them.

Now, let's dive into the techniques for guiding your subjects to use their hands expressively. It's all about creating a comfortable space where they can express themselves freely. Start by engaging in a conversation about their cultural background and personal stories. This dialogue can be incredibly insightful and can guide you in choosing hand gestures that are both meaningful and authentic. For instance, if your subject is of Indian descent, they might share stories of traditional dances or festivals where certain hand gestures are symbolic. Use these stories as a springboard to incorporate those gestures into your session. It's about making the photo session interactive and personal, turning it into a collaborative storytelling process.

But how about adding even more depth and context to these portraits? This is where cultural artifacts come into play. Integrating cultural artifacts into hand poses enriches your portraits' visual appeal and deepens the narrative. Picture a musician holding an ancient flute, their fingers gracefully positioned over the holes, ready to breathe life into a melody passed down through generations. Or a calligrapher, their hands poised elegantly over a parchment, brush in hand, connecting with centuries-old art forms. These artifacts act as bridges, linking the individual to their cultural heritage and enhancing the storytelling aspect of your portraits. They provide a context that enriches the viewer's understanding and appreciation of the culture being portrayed.

Moreover, the real magic happens when hands become the narrators of personal and communal histories. Each line, scar, or gesture holds a story, a piece of history that is uniquely theirs yet universally resonant. For example, the hands of a potter from Pueblo, stained with the clay of the very earth their ancestors walked upon, can tell a profound story about tradition, survival, and art. Or consider the hands of a grandmother, her fingers wrapped around a vintage locket, each wrinkle narrating tales of love, loss, and life lessons. These stories, told through hands, allow us to capture more than just images; they enable us to preserve histories and share them with the world. Through your lens, hands become a canvas, painting stories of cultures, battles fought, victories won, and legacies passed on.

In essence, cultural portrait photography is not just about capturing faces; it's about capturing the essence of identities, with hands acting as powerful conduits of personal and cultural narratives. It's about turning each portrait session into a journey of discovery, a celebration of heritage, and a preservation of history, one hand gesture at a time. So next time you're framing a shot, remember, the hands are not just part of the portrait; they are the heart of the story. Let them speak, let them narrate, let them be the bridge that connects the personal to the universal. Through your camera, their stories can resonate across cultures and generations, painting a picture richer and deeper than ever imagined.

The Evolution of Hand Poses in Art History

Let's take a stroll down memory lane, but not just any lane—this one's lined with the masterpieces of art history, each telling a tale not just with faces and landscapes, but with the silent poetry of hands. From the rigid, symbolic gestures of medieval paintings to the expressive, fluid forms in modern art, the evolution of hand poses is like a visual symphony, echoing the cultural and societal shifts of each era. It's a fascinating journey that shows us not only how art has mirrored the changes in society but also how these ancient cues still ripple through the lens of contemporary photography.

Historical Context

Imagine the stiff, almost awkward hand gestures in Byzantine art, where every finger position had a theological significance, a stark contrast to the relaxed and naturalistic hands found in Renaissance paintings, which aimed to capture the beauty and fluidity of human form. This shift wasn't just an artistic revolution; it was a cultural awakening, reflecting a society that was beginning to prize humanism and the study of classical antiquity. Fast forward to the Baroque period, and you see hands that are dynamic, dramatic, full of movement and emotion, mirroring the turbulent times of the 17th century with its deep religious and political changes. Each of these shifts in hand posing styles in art history wasn't just about new aesthetic preferences; they were reflections of the societal pulses of their times, indicators of broader cultural shifts and human experiences.

Influence on Contemporary Photography

Now, how does this all play into the clicks and flashes of contemporary photography? Quite significantly, actually! Modern photographers, whether they realize it or not, are conversing with these historical hand poses, sometimes echoing them, sometimes challenging them. For instance, the delicate, detailed hand gestures in Rococo art inspire wedding photographers aiming for that airy, romantic feel in their shots. On the flip side, the bold, exaggerated poses of Expressionist art can be seen in the edgy, impactful shots of fashion photography. It's like having a dialogue with the past, where each shot weaves a bit of history with modern narratives, creating images that are rich with layers of time and meaning.

Iconic Hand Poses

And oh, the stories that iconic hand poses from art history can tell! Take Da Vinci's "The Last Supper," where each apostle's hands reveal their inner turmoil and foretell their fate, a masterclass in using hand gestures to enhance narrative depth. Or Michelangelo's "Creation of Adam" on the Sistine Chapel ceiling, where the near-touching hands of God and Adam have become a universal symbol of creation and existential connection. These iconic hand poses are not just frozen in time; they inspire contemporary photographers to infuse their works with similar depth and symbolism, encouraging a photographic style that's both evocative and narratively rich. It's about drawing from the old to create something new, something that resonates with today's viewers yet whispers tales of the past.

Blending Tradition and Innovation

So, how do you marry tradition with innovation in your photography? Start by studying these historical hand poses and understand the context and emotions they were meant to convey. Then, play with these elements in your framing—perhaps positioning a subject's hands in a way that nods to classical paintings but in a setting that's starkly modern. It's about creating a visual bridge between the past and the present, where historical gestures meet modern contexts, producing images that are rich in heritage and fresh in perspective. This blending not only enriches your photographic vocabulary but also gives your images a layered quality, making them visually compelling and intellectually engaging.

As you explore the vast gallery of art history, let the timeless gestures guide you, inspire you, and sometimes even challenge you. With each click of your camera, you're not just capturing a moment; you're weaving a thread between the now and the then, between your vision and the visions of those who painted, sculpted, and created before you. It's a beautiful continuum, where the hands not only tell where we've been but also hint at where we're going. So keep those eyes on the past, but let your camera capture the future.

Bridging Generations: Hand Poses that Tell Stories

Imagine capturing a moment that transcends time, where the past meets the present in the simple clasp of hands between a grandmother and her grandchild. This is the power of generational hand gestures, a visual narrative that bridges ages and eras in a single frame. These gestures serve as a living archive of familial bonds and cultural continuity, offering a glimpse into the personal legacies that weave through generations. When you photograph a centenarian with hands clasped over a walking stick, those same hands once cradled a newborn, threw stones into rivers as a child, and exchanged wedding rings. Each wrinkle tells a tale of decades lived, of joys and challenges weathered. Capturing these gestures isn't just about snapping elderly hands; it's about honoring the life they've led and the traditions they pass on. It's a profound reminder that every hand gesture carries the weight of history and the touch of ancestors long gone.

Now, let's talk about family portraits, but forget those stiff, everyone-look-at-the-camera shots. Instead, think of family portraits that tell deeper stories through hands. A great start is to have family members engage in a common activity that involves their hands. Maybe they're making pasta from an old family recipe, with flour-dusted hands kneading the dough. Or perhaps they're planting a new tree in their backyard, hands covered in soil, together laying the roots for future growth. These activities do more than just keep hands busy; they create a narrative about shared traditions and values passed down through generations. The hands become the focal point of the portrait, telling stories of heritage and legacy, of the ties that bind long after the photo is taken. It's about capturing those candid moments where hands are not just in motion, but emotion, crafting a visual story that will be cherished for generations to come.

Photography also plays a pivotal role in documenting cultural shifts. Hands can be a powerful lens through which to observe and record these changes. Consider how the handshakes of businesswomen in a corporate boardroom might signify the shifting roles of women in sectors traditionally dominated by men. Or how the hands of young people, adorned with technology and gadgets, contrast with the rugged, calloused hands of older generations. These contrasts not only highlight the evolution of societal roles and norms but also underscore the consistencies that remain. By focusing on hands within different cultural contexts, you can create a visual dialogue between the old and the new, capturing the dynamic nature of cultural evolution. It's about showing not just where we are heading, but also where we have been, and how every generation shapes the next.

Encouraging personal narratives through hand poses takes this a step further, turning each photograph into a personal document, a testament of individual and collective histories. When you ask someone to show you how they hold their tools of trade or their instruments of art, you're inviting them to share a part of their story. For instance, a musician's hands on the strings of a worn guitar can tell of years of self-taught skill and nights of soulful melodies. Or a baker's hands, dusted with flour, shaping dough precisely as their grandmother taught them, can speak of traditions that nourish more than just bodies.

These stories, told through hands, are profoundly personal yet universally relatable. They remind us that our hands are tools of action, but also of expression, capable of telling our deepest stories without uttering a single word.

In essence, when you choose to focus on hands in your photography, you're not just taking pictures; you're preserving histories. You're capturing the essence of personal journeys and cultural evolutions, one gesture at a time. So next time you lift your camera, look beyond the obvious. See the hands, see the stories they hold, and let them speak through your lens.

Navigating Cultural Sensitivities with Creativity and Respect

When it comes to the intricate dance of capturing culturally sensitive hand gestures, think of yourself as both an artist and a diplomat. Balancing creative expression with respect for cultural sensitivities isn't just about avoiding blunders—it's about crafting images that honor and celebrate the diversity of human expression. So, how do you keep your creative spark alive without stepping on cultural toes? It's a bit like being a chef who knows just how much spice to add to a dish without overpowering its flavors. For photographers, this means understanding the cultural implications behind certain hand gestures and finding ways to incorporate them into your work that enhance, rather than exploit or misrepresent, the subjects and their heritage.

Imagine you're shooting in a locale where certain hand signs, which might be benign back home, are considered taboo. Instead of forcing your usual style, why not let the local culture guide your creativity? This could mean asking your subjects to demonstrate hand gestures that are significant to their cultural rituals or everyday communications. Photographing these authentic gestures not only adds a layer of depth and authenticity to your work but also respects the cultural norms. It's about creating art that's as informed as it is beautiful, ensuring that every hand gesture you capture tells a true story of the people and cultures portrayed.

However, even the most well-intentioned photographers can run into challenges when navigating cultural sensitivities. One common hurdle is the risk of misinterpretation—what if your artistic vision accidentally misrepresents a cultural symbol? Here's where your background homework comes into play. Before you even frame your shot, spend time understanding the symbolic meanings of hand gestures in that culture. Engage with local experts or guides who can provide insights into the dos and don'ts. Think of it as gathering ingredients for a recipe; the better your ingredients, the better your dish turns out. And always review your images with a local eye before publishing them—this not only polishes your work but also safeguards against potential cultural missteps.

Ethical considerations are the backbone of culturally sensitive photography. Every time you aim your camera at a subject, you're in a position of power. How you choose to represent your subjects can have a profound impact on how they're perceived by the world. This is especially crucial when photographing hand gestures that might hold religious or cultural significance.

Always approach these situations with humility and the intent to learn, not just to capture. Seek permission where necessary, and be transparent about how and where your images will be used. This ethical approach not only ensures respect and integrity in your interactions but also enriches your work with genuine respect and appreciation for the cultures you're documenting.

Fostering cultural exchange through photography is about more than just taking pictures—it's about opening dialogues and building bridges. Each image you create can serve as a window into a world different from your own, offering viewers a chance to explore, understand, and appreciate other cultures through the universal language of visual art. By focusing on hand gestures, you highlight the unique ways people communicate and express themselves across the globe. This not only enriches your portfolio but also contributes to a broader understanding and respect among cultures, showcasing the beauty and diversity of human expression in its many forms.

In wrapping up this exploration into the culturally rich world of hand gestures, remember that your camera is a powerful tool for cultural storytelling. Use it wisely, with respect and creativity, and you will not only capture images with great visual impact but also with profound cultural respect and significance. As we close this chapter, let these lessons in cultural sensitivity inspire you to approach your next photography project with a renewed perspective, ready to explore and celebrate the rich tapestry of human gestures and expressions that await. As we turn the page, let's carry forward the ethos of respect and creativity into every shot we frame, every story we tell.

Chapter 6: Setting Your Work Apart: Unique Selling Points and Final Touches

Ever felt like your photography was just one star in a vast galaxy, struggling to shine a little brighter? Well, gear up because we're about to turbocharge your work with some interstellar magic that's sure to make your photos pop in the cosmic chaos of the photography world. This chapter isn't just about tweaking your exposure or mastering the rule of thirds—nope, we're diving into the high-tech, high-fun world of QR codes and how they can transform your photography from flat to phantasmagorical!

Incorporating QR Codes for Interactive Learning Experiences

Enhancing Educational Content

Imagine this: You're flipping through a photography book or scrolling through an online gallery and bam! You spot a QR code next to a photo that just screams mystery and intrigue.

You whip out your phone, scan the code, and suddenly you're watching a behind-the-scenes video that shows exactly how that shot was captured. Magic, right? Embedding QR codes in your photography books or on your website can turn a static viewing experience into an interactive treasure hunt. Each scan brings your audience closer to your creative process, peeling back layers of your work they might never see otherwise. It's like giving them a backstage pass to your most guarded secrets, but without the risk of them tripping over any cables.

Engagement Through Technology

But why stop at educational content? QR codes can be your golden ticket to boosting engagement. They're like those fun little 'Press Here' buttons in kids' books, but for grown-ups with gadgets. By embedding QR codes, you invite viewers to interact with your work in real-time. Scan here to vote for your favorite photo; scan there to post a selfie with my artwork in the background; scan everywhere because each code can link to different online challenges, quizzes, polls—you name it. This level of interaction doesn't just keep your audience entertained; it makes them participants in your photographic journey. They're no longer passive viewers; they're active explorers, engaged and invested in your work, which boosts not only your visibility but also their loyalty. Who knew tiny pixelated squares could be so powerful?

Creative Implementation

Now, let's get those creative juices flowing. QR codes don't have to be bland and purely functional. Oh no, they can be part of the art! Imagine integrating a QR code into the artwork itself, where it complements the composition or adds a layer of mystery. Maybe it's hidden in the shadows of a noir-style portrait or woven into the intricate patterns of a landscape shot. You could even create a scavenger hunt where each code leads to another, each photo unlocking the next part of a serialized story you've photographed. The possibilities are as limitless as your creativity, turning each photo into an interactive experience that tantalizes the senses and the intellect.

Tracking Engagement

And because we're not just shooting in the dark here, let's talk metrics. QR codes can be a goldmine of data, providing insights into which aspects of your work resonate most with your audience. Every scan is a direct feedback loop from viewer to photographer, giving you hard data on what excites your audience, what makes them tick, and what keeps them coming back for more. This isn't just valuable for stroking your ego— it's crucial for shaping your future projects and marketing strategies. By understanding your audience's engagement, you're better equipped to tailor your work to meet their interests, ensuring your photography stays relevant and riveting.

So, whether you're a seasoned pro looking to spice up your portfolio or a budding photographer eager to make your mark, consider the humble QR code—your new best friend in the digital age. Sure, it's a simple tool, but with some creativity, it can open up a world of interaction, education, and engagement that takes your photography to a whole new level of awesome. Let those QR codes sprinkle a little digital magic on your work, and watch as your photographs transform from mere images to interactive adventures that captivate, educate, and inspire.

Building an Online Community for Continuous Feedback

Foundation of Community Building

So, you want to turn your solo photography gig into a buzzing beehive of interaction and growth? Well, step right up to the digital age, where building an online community of photography enthusiasts is not just smart; it's essential for tapping into a wellspring of creativity and support. Imagine a place where each photo you post sparks a conversation, where feedback flows as freely as coffee at a midnight editing session. Creating this community is like hosting the world's biggest dinner party, but instead of food, you're serving up fresh snaps and hot takes on photography.

Start by setting the table with a clear purpose for your community. Is it to refine skills, share projects, or maybe crowdsource photography wisdom? Whatever it is, make it clear because, just like at any good party, people want to know what they're walking into. Next up, establish some ground rules. Just as you wouldn't let guests throw food at a dinner party, make sure everyone knows what's cool and what's not in your community. Encourage a culture of respect, where feedback is constructive and everyone's views are valued. Remember, a safe environment is a productive environment.

Finally, be the host with the most. Engage actively with your members, spark discussions, and maybe throw in a few challenges or live critique sessions to keep the energy high. Your role is to guide the conversation, cheer on improvements, and step in when things go off track. It's about nurturing a space where everyone can grow, including you.

Platforms for Community Engagement

Choosing the right platform to host your community is like picking the perfect venue for your party. You need somewhere that's not only spacious and welcoming but also easy to use and accessible. For photographers, platforms that let you showcase your visual work with ease are key. Think Instagram for its massive, visually-inclined user base and user-friendly interface. It's like the hip downtown bar where everyone wants to hang out. Then there's Facebook, with its group functionalities that are perfect for fostering discussions and sharing a variety of content, from albums to videos to quick posts. It's the community hall of social media —traditional but functional.

But don't overlook specialized platforms like Flickr or 500px, like exclusive clubs for photography aficionados. These platforms offer space to display high-quality images and robust communities where feedback, discussions, and connections are all in a day's work. Whichever platform you choose, make sure it aligns with the needs of your community and the nature of your interactions. It should be a place where your members can easily engage, share, and feel part of a vibrant photographer's hub.

Encouraging Constructive Criticism

Now, let's talk about nurturing a culture of constructive criticism because let's face it—no one grows in an echo chamber of endless praise. Start by setting an example; be the critique-giver you wish to see in your community. Offer thoughtful, specific feedback rather than generic 'nice shot' comments. Explain why you like a certain aspect of a photo or suggest how a different angle or setting might enhance it. It's about adding value, not just noise.

Next, encourage your community members to think critically about their feedback. Maybe introduce a critique template or guidelines like the 'sandwich method'—a piece of positive feedback, followed by constructive criticism, and topped with another positive note. It's like serving up criticism with a side of kindness. Also, consider hosting regular critique threads or virtual meet-ups where members can get real-time feedback in a supportive environment. It's about creating a learning culture where growth is part of the game.

Leveraging Community Insights

Last but not least, let's not forget that feedback is a two-way street. The insights you gather from your community are like nuggets of gold in improving your craft and understanding your audience better. Pay attention to the trends in the feedback you receive. Are certain themes or techniques in your work receiving more attention or praise? Use this data to steer your creative endeavors and refine your style.

Additionally, keep an eye on the discussions and most frequently asked questions within your community. These can guide the content you create, perhaps inspiring blog posts, tutorial videos, or even new photography projects that address common challenges or interests. It's about using the community not just as a sounding board but as a compass that guides your creative journey.

By building this dynamic, interactive community, you're setting the stage for not just better photography but for richer, more meaningful connections in the world of photography. It's about taking your passion for photography and multiplying it, creating a space where ideas, feedback, and creativity flourish. Now, go forth and build your tribe, one photo, one critique, and one connection at a time. Let the shutter clicks echo through the digital corridors of your new community, marking the beginning of something truly spectacular.

Ethical Considerations in Hand Posing and Photography

Imagine you're all set for a shoot that you know could be your next big portfolio piece. The lighting, the ambiance, everything feels just right. But as you guide your model to pose, have you paused to consider the implications of your creative decisions? Let's face it, navigating the ethical labyrinth in photography, especially when it involves nuanced elements like hand posing, can sometimes feel like trying to solve a Rubik's Cube blindfolded. But fret not! By sticking to a few ethical guidelines, you can ensure your work is not only stunning but also respectful and responsible.

Respecting Subject Consent

First things first, let's talk consent. It's the bedrock of all ethical photography. This isn't just about getting a nod before you start snapping away. It's about fully informing your subjects about how their images and, specifically, their hand gestures will be used. Will their hands be framing their face in a way that suggests a certain emotion? Are you asking them to make a gesture that has specific cultural connotations? Clarity here is key. You should aim for an understanding as clear as a high-resolution image. This means discussing the intent behind your shots and any potential for these images to be distributed or displayed. Remember, a model's comfort and understanding of how their hands—their personal tools of expression—are portrayed, can make or break the trust necessary for a successful shoot.

Cultural Sensitivity and Appropriation

Now, onto the slippery slopes of cultural sensitivity and appropriation. It's crucial to tread carefully when incorporating hand gestures that carry cultural weight. What looks cool and edgy in your frame might be a sacred symbol in another culture. The last thing any photographer wants is to turn their art into a case study in cultural insensitivity. So, how do you avoid this? Research, research, and more research. Before you decide to replicate that cool gesture you saw in a travel documentary or a foreign film, dive deep into its origins consultants or tap into resources that can offer insights into the and meanings. Engage with cultural gestures you wish to portray. This isn't just about avoiding backlash; it's about respecting and honoring the rich tapestries of cultures that you bring into your work. Plus, it adds a layer of depth and authenticity to your photos that can't be matched by mere aesthetics alone.

Privacy and Anonymity

Photography often captures more than just images; it captures vulnerabilities. This is where considerations around privacy and anonymity come into play, especially in sensitive or personal contexts. Suppose you're documenting a heartfelt moment at a shelter or a sensitive cultural ceremony. In cases like this, the decision to anonymize your subjects can be as crucial as the decision to press the shutter. Sometimes, showing less reveals more. Perhaps you focus solely on the hands, capturing the essence of the moment without exposing faces. This approach not only protects your subjects' identities but also invites viewers to focus intimately on the story told through the hands. It's about finding that sweet spot where you respect your subjects' privacy while still telling a compelling story through your lens.

Ethical Editing Practices

Finally, let's pixel-peep into the world of post-processing— where magic and misdemeanor can happen. Ethical editing is about being true to your vision without distorting the truth. When it comes to hand posing, subtle enhancements are fine, but fundamentally altering the gesture to convey something it was not can mislead viewers and misrepresent your subjects. Keep edits realistic and responsible. If you're enhancing contrast or sharpness, great! But if you're digitally manipulating an image to change the narrative or the cultural context of the hand gesture, you might want to pause and reconsider. Your editing software is a powerful tool—use it to enhance, not deceive.

Navigating the ethical considerations in hand posing and photography can seem daunting, but it's really about sticking to a simple principle: respect—for your craft, your subjects, and the cultures you portray. With this as your guiding light, you can ensure that your photography not only captures eyes but also respects hearts and minds.

Utilizing Technology: Apps and Tools for Perfect Hand Poses

Software and Applications

Alright, let's talk tech magic! Imagine you're on a shoot, and you've got the perfect scene set up—golden hour light, a breeze gently tousling your subject's hair. But then, the age-old question pops up: "What do I do with my hands?" Instead of diving into the deep abyss of manual posing books, whip out your smartphone because, believe it or not, there's an app for that! Today's market is bustling with software and applications designed specifically to help photographers nail those tricky hand poses. These aren't just your run-of-the-mill photo editing tools; we're talking about specialized apps that serve as virtual posing coaches.

For instance, picture an app that features a library of hand poses ranging from natural to avant-garde, each accompanied by tips on when and how to use them effectively. You could scroll through, find the perfect pose, and even show it directly to your model—no more awkward hand-flapping trying to explain what you mean. But it gets better. Some apps come equipped with features that let you tweak the virtual hands' positioning, adjusting the fingers' curl or the wrist's angle, so you can experiment and visualize the perfect pose before you even ask your model to lift a finger. This hands-on (pun intended!) approach not only saves time but also sparks creativity, allowing you to try out poses you might not have thought of organically. It's like having a little hand-posing wizard in your pocket, ready to cast a spell whenever you hit a creative block.

Technology in Planning

Now, let's zoom out for a second and consider the bigger picture—planning your shoots. Technology has galloped in from the future, bringing tools that make visualizing and planning your shoots a breeze. Imagine software that lets you create detailed storyboards or mood boards, not just with sample images, but with interactive, adjustable hand poses. You could map out every shot beforehand, deciding exactly how your model should position their hands to convey the emotion or story you're aiming for.

This kind of tech isn't just about prettifying your plan; it's a strategic tool. By meticulously planning the hand poses, you ensure consistency and coherence throughout your shoot, which is especially crucial if you're working on a thematic series or a narrative project. Tools like these often come with features that allow you to share your plans with your team or clients, ensuring everyone is on the same page, literally and figuratively. It's like conducting an orchestra where everyone knows their cues—your makeup artist knows just how dramatic to go, your lighting technician knows just where to cast shadows to accentuate those hands, and your model knows just the right angle to hold. This harmony, enabled by technology, can transform a good shoot into a masterpiece where every element sings in unison.

Augmented Reality for Posing

Stepping into the realm of sci-fi (but totally real), let's talk about augmented reality (AR). AR in photography, especially for posing, is like having a cheat sheet that only you can see. There are AR apps now that allow you to overlay virtual poses onto your live camera feed. So, you could be aiming your camera at your model and see on your screen a ghost image of the pose you're trying to achieve. It's like playing a game of "match the pose," except the stakes are high and the outcomes are stunning photographs.

This technology is particularly useful when trying to achieve complex hand poses requiring precise angles or alignments. It reduces guesswork and multiple shots, allowing you to nail the pose quickly and efficiently. Plus, it's a fantastic tool for education and training. What better way to demonstrate if you're teaching a workshop on hand posing than with real-time, AR-guided examples? It's an immersive learning experience that can significantly enhance understanding and retention of the techniques you're teaching.

Feedback and Analysis Tools

Last but definitely not least, let's delve into the analytical side of things. Feedback and analysis tools are the unsung heroes in the tech ensemble. These tools can analyze your photos post-shoot and give you feedback on everything from composition to the effectiveness of poses. Some tools even use AI to suggest adjustments or improvements, offering an objective eye that can catch things you might have missed.

Imagine finishing a shoot and running your photos through a software that highlights which hand poses worked best in terms of viewer engagement or aesthetic balance. This feedback isn't just useful; it's gold dust for refining your technique and evolving your style. It's like having a coach who's part cheerleader, part critic, but all geared towards making your next shoot better than your last. These tools often come with analytics dashboards that show you trends and patterns in your work, helping you understand your own style better and make informed decisions about future projects. It's not just feedback; it's a roadmap to becoming a better photographer.

So, there you have it—your tech toolkit for taking hand posing from good to mind-blowingly great. Whether it's through innovative apps, strategic planning software, AR magic, or analytical tools, technology offers a treasure trove of ways to enhance your photographic process and product.

Dive in, experiment, and watch as your photography reaches new heights of precision and creativity.

The Future of Hand Posing: Trends to Watch Out For

In the dynamic dance of digital and analog, where photography constantly evolves at the beat of technological innovations and shifting cultural landscapes, hand posing too whirls to its own rhythm, forecasting trends that could redefine how we communicate visually. As we peer through the viewfinder into the future, a fascinating panorama unfolds, showcasing emerging trends in hand posing that might just set the stage for the next wave of photographic expression.

One intriguing trend on the rise is the blending of traditional hand gestures with contemporary flair, creating a visual fusion that bridges generations and geographies. This trend is not merely about aesthetics; it reflects a deeper cultural shift towards global interconnectedness. Young photographers, armed with global access via social media, are increasingly experimenting with hand poses that have historic or cultural significance in other parts of the world. This not only enriches their artistic repertoire but also fosters a more inclusive visual dialogue that transcends borders. It's as if each photograph becomes a handshake between the old and the new, the here and the elsewhere. Imagine a fashion shoot where a model uses a hand gesture from classical Indian dance to express grace, or a street portrait capturing a handshake that blends a traditional Moroccan greeting with a hip-hop fist bump.

These are the kinds of hybrid expressions that could dominate future portfolios, offering fresh narratives woven from the diverse threads of our global tapestry.

On the tech front, the integration of AI and AR into the realm of hand posing is not just exciting—it's revolutionary. Artificial intelligence, with its ability to learn and adapt, is poised to offer personalized suggestions for hand poses based on the mood, theme, or even the cultural context of the shoot. Picture an AI assistant that, after analyzing thousands of images, can suggest the perfect hand gesture to evoke a sense of longing or jubilation in your portrait work. Meanwhile, augmented reality could take this a step further by allowing photographers to superimpose these AI-generated hand poses onto their live view, ensuring the pose is just right before the shutter clicks. This could be particularly groundbreaking for educational purposes, providing new photographers with a virtual hand-posing tutor that guides them through complex gestures step-by-step. As these technologies mature, they could become as commonplace in a photographer's toolkit as the camera itself, making advanced hand posing accessible to everyone and dynamically changing the learning curve in photography education.

Cultural norms and their evolution also play a pivotal role in shaping the future of hand posing. As societies become more aware and sensitive to cultural appropriation, photographers must navigate the delicate balance between inspiration and appropriation. This doesn't mean shying away from cultural expressions but rather engaging with them more thoughtfully. The future might see more collaborations where photographers work directly with cultural ambassadors or experts to incorporate traditional gestures into modern photography authentically. This respectful approach not only enriches the artistic authenticity but also educates the audience, turning each photo into a conduit for cultural appreciation and understanding.

Sustainability in photography, especially regarding the portrayal of subjects and the environmental impact of photo shoots, is becoming a pressing concern. Ethical considerations that were once peripheral are moving to the forefront of photographic practices. Photographers are beginning to embrace more eco-friendly practices, from the digital backdrop to the reduction of travel and the use of sustainable materials in their shoots. With hand posing, this might translate into more localized shooting, using hand models from the community that reduce the carbon footprint associated with flying models from different parts of the world. Moreover, the ethical portrayal of subjects, particularly in how their cultural and personal identities are represented through hand gestures, is gaining attention. This shift towards ethical and sustainable practices not only aligns with global efforts to combat climate change but also enhances the social responsibility of the photographic community.

As we adjust our lenses and focus on the horizons of hand posing, these trends hint at a future where photography continues to evolve as a craft and a communication medium. From integrating cutting-edge technologies to the deepening respect for cultural expressions and sustainable practices, the future of hand posing is as promising as it is exciting. Each snapshot and gesture holds the potential not just to capture a moment but to tell a story, educate, and inspire, bridging the past and the future in the palm of our hands. As these trends unfold and gain momentum, they beckon photographers to not only witness but also shape the evolving narrative of visual expression.

Crafting Your Signature Style with Hand Poses

Defining Your Style

Picture this: you're at a gallery, and you can spot a Van Gogh from a mile away—not just because of the starry skies or sunflowers but because of his unmistakable brushstrokes. Now, wouldn't it be something if people could recognize your photographs just by the way hands are posed? Crafting a signature style with hand poses isn't just about standing out in a crowded field; it's about imprinting your personal artistic stamp on every frame you shoot. To start, think about what moves you in photographs. Is it the soft, tender touch in a family portrait, or the dramatic, sculpted lines in a fashion shoot? Begin by experimenting with these elements in your own work. Maybe you start using more dynamic hand gestures in your portraits to add a layer of intensity, or perhaps you play with subtle hand placements that tell a deeper story without words. The key is consistency—once you find that 'hand pose' that feels like you, use it, refine it, and make it your trademark. Over time, this consistent element in your photos will become your style signature, as recognizable as your own handwriting.

Inspiration and Originality

Now, let's talk about keeping your inspiration fresh while staying original. It's easy to fall into the trap of copying hand poses that you see in popular photos, but where's the fun in that? Instead, let those images spark your creativity, not dictate it. Dive into the history of art, study the gestures in classical paintings, or observe the way people move their hands in everyday life—there's your gold mine of inspiration. Start integrating these observations into your photography. Maybe you notice the way a baker kneads dough and see a pose that would look perfect in a culinary lifestyle shoot. Or perhaps the elegant hand gestures of a classical dancer inspire you to experiment with more fluid, expressive poses in your fashion work. The trick is to take these inspirations and twist them into something that screams 'you.' It's not about reinvention from scratch but about personal reinterpretation that sets your work apart.

Consistency Across Work

Maintaining consistency in your hand posing can be a game-changer for your brand identity. Think of it as your visual calling card. Whether you're shooting for a magazine, a personal project, or a commercial client, incorporating your signature hand pose style can make your work instantly recognizable. This doesn't mean every photo needs to look the same—far from it. It's about weaving a common thread through your diverse projects that mark each one as unmistakably yours. For instance, if your signature style involves whimsical, playful hand poses, find ways to introduce elements of this, even in more serious shoots. It could be as subtle as the way a model rests their hands on a lapel or as obvious as a full-frame shot focusing on the hands. This consistency strengthens your brand and builds a coherent portfolio that tells potential clients, 'This is what I do, and I do it well.'

Evolving Your Style

Lastly, let's consider the evolution of your style. Just as you grow and change, so too should your photography. Embracing new influences and experimenting with different techniques is the lifeblood of artistic growth. Maybe you take a workshop on dance photography and learn a whole new set of dynamic hand poses that you want to incorporate into your editorial work. Or perhaps you're inspired by a period drama to try more ornate, vintage-style hand gestures in your next project. Welcome these changes; play with them until they feel like part of your artistic voice. Remember, evolving your style isn't about hopping on every trend—it's about absorbing new ideas and weaving them into the fabric of your unique artistic expression. This evolution keeps your work fresh and exciting, not just for your audience but for you as well. As you explore new horizons in hand posing, you keep pushing the boundaries of what you can create with your camera and your imagination. Keep experimenting, keep learning, and watch as your signature style grows and flourishes, marking every photograph with the unmistakable stamp of your creative spirit.

Beyond the Lens: Hand Poses in Digital and Mixed Media Art

When you think about art, it's not just the canvas, the brush-strokes, or even the colors that paint the full picture. Often, it's the hands that bring the magic to life, shaping the clay, strumming the guitar, or in our case, clicking the shutter. But what happens when you take those hands from a photograph and blend them into the kaleidoscopic world of digital and mixed media art? Well, you're in for a treat—a spectacular fusion where photography meets digital wizardry, creating a realm where anything is possible.

Integrating Photography and Digital Art

Let's kick things off by diving into the seamless integration of hand poses from your photographs into digital and mixed-media art projects. Picture this: you have a stunning photo of a ballet dancer, her hands expressing grace and poise as they cut through the air. Now, reimagine those hands in a digital landscape—perhaps as part of a surreal collage where each finger morphs into a feather, blurring the lines between human and bird, reality and fantasy. This is where traditional photography meets its wild, imaginative cousin, digital art. By using software tools like Adobe Photoshop or open-source alternatives like GIMP, you can manipulate and merge photographic elements with digital textures, graphics, and more. The key here is to maintain the integrity and the expressive power of the hand while guiding it into new, uncharted territories of artistic expression. It's about creating a dialogue between your photographic eye and your digital art instincts, each one feeding into and enhancing the other.

Techniques for Blending Mediums

Now, blending these mediums to make them sing in harmony is an art in itself. Start with the basics: layering. Think of your artwork as a delicious lasagna—each layer adds depth and flavor, combining to create something extraordinary. Use layers in your digital art software to stack different elements, adjust- ing their opacity and blending modes to see how they interact. Maybe the translucent silhouette of a hand overlays perfectly over a stormy seascape, suggesting a struggle or a conquest. Play around with filters and effects—transform a hand into a glowing neon sign or a shadowy, mysterious figure. The trick is to experiment with these tools to find the perfect balance that enhances the hand's expressiveness without overwhelming it. And don't forget about color! Adjusting hues and saturation can turn a natural hand pose into a vivid, otherworldly gesture.

Expanding Artistic Expression

Incorporating hand poses into your digital and mixed media art isn't just about aesthetics; it's a powerful way to expand your storytelling. Hands can express so many emotions— anger, peace, desperation, or joy. By bringing these into digital art, you open up a plethora of ways to tell stories. For instance, a series of artworks that depicts hands in various states of openness and closure can metaphorically represent themes of acceptance and rejection. Or a mixed media piece where hands are reaching out from different corners towards a central, glowing orb could symbolize a quest for knowledge or enlightenment. Each hand pose holds the potential to convey a narrative, and by blending it into digital art, you amplify its voice, allowing it to speak in colors, textures, and forms that photography alone might not achieve.

Creating a Portfolio that Highlights Your Mastery of Hand Posing

Curating Your Best Work

Think of your portfolio as your greatest hits album; every photo should be a chart-topper. When it comes to showcasing your mastery of hand posing, the key is not just to throw in every hand-focused shot you've ever taken but to select those that truly sing. Start by laying out all your candidates. Now, be ruthless—only the photos where the hand poses add a clear, compelling element to the image should make the cut. Look for diversity in expressions, contexts, and emotions. That shot of a grandmother's hands wrapped around a young grandchild's, imparting wisdom? In. The fashion model's hands striking an avant-garde pose that complements their attire? Definitely in. This selective process ensures that every image in your portfolio contributes to a narrative of versatility and skill, proving that you're not just taking pictures; you're crafting stories, one hand pose at a time.

Next, consider the flow. Just like a good album has a mix of upbeat tracks and ballads, your portfolio should balance dynamic and subtle hand poses to show your range. Start with a few strong, eye-catching images to grab attention, then take the viewer on a visual journey through different styles and moods. Each transition should feel natural, not jarring, leading them seamlessly from one theme to another. This thoughtful curation not only highlights your technical skills but also your artistic sensibility, showing that you know just how to feature hands in a way that enhances the story without overpowering the scene.

Presentation Platforms

Now, where to showcase this stunning portfolio? In today's digital age, you've got a plethora of platforms to choose from, each with its unique flair. Traditional print portfolios are still a hit for that tactile, personal touch during face-to-face meetings. There's something about flipping through glossy pages that digital screens just can't match. But don't stop there. Digital platforms offer a broader reach and the flexibility to update your work easily. A well-designed website can serve as your portfolio's home base, with categories for different types of hand posing—commercial, editorial, personal work, you name it.

Don't overlook the power of social media platforms like In-Instagram or Pinterest, which are visual gold mines for pho-photographers. These platforms allow not just for presentation but also for interaction. You can receive immediate feedback, gauge what resonates with your audience, and tweak your portfolio accordingly. Plus, these platforms can act as teasers, drawing viewers to your main website for the full experience. Remember, each platform has its vibe and audience. Tailor your presentation to fit the platform's strengths, ensuring your portfolio always appears in its best light.

Narrative Through Hand Poses

Creating a narrative in your portfolio through hand poses is like writing a visual novel where each photo is a chapter. The hands are your characters—what story do they tell? Maybe it's a tale of craftsmanship through the hands of various artisans, or a story of human emotions conveyed through gestures of love, despair, and joy. This thematic approach can be incredibly compelling, giving your portfolio a cohesive storyline that engages viewers and keeps them flipping to the next page (or scrolling to the next image).

To build this narrative, each image should contribute to the overarching theme, yet stand strong on its own. It's about finding that sweet spot where individual excellence meets collective coherence. Think about the order of images—how does one lead to the next? How does the emotion or message evolve? This isn't just about displaying skills; it's about taking your viewer on a journey that leaves them moved, impressed, and wanting more.

Gaining Visibility

Finally, what good is a killer portfolio if it's hidden away in a drawer? Visibility is key. Start local; participate in photography exhibitions or fairs where you can display your work and network face-to-face. These events are fantastic for getting direct feedback and connecting with potential clients or collaborators.

But also think bigger. Online photography contests can be a great platform to gain international exposure. Winning or even getting shortlisted can serve as a significant endorsement of your skills.

Leverage social media for all it's worth. Regular posts, engaging captions, and interaction with your followers can help build a loyal audience who will champion your work. Consider collaborations with other artists or influencers, which can introduce your portfolio to a whole new crowd. And don't forget about the power of SEO for your online portfolio. Use relevant keywords, maintain an active blog, and ensure your website is as search-engine friendly as possible. This behind-the-scenes work can make a big difference in how easily people find you and your work online.

Crafting a portfolio that effectively highlights your mastery of hand posing is an art form in itself. It's about more than just showing what you can do; it's about creating a narrative, engaging your audience emotionally, and strategically placing your work where it can shine brightest. Treat your portfolio as a living entity, continually evolving and adapting, just as you do as a photographer. With these strategies, you're not just putting your work out there; you're ensuring it leaves a mark.

As we wrap up this chapter, remember that each photo you select, each story you tell, and each platform you choose plays a crucial role in defining your photographic identity. Your portfolio is your voice in the vast, bustling world of photography— make it loud, make it clear, and most importantly, make it yours. Now, armed with these insights, go forth and create artistic photographs that best showcase your creative, photographic abilities.

Conclusion

Well, folks, we've reached the grand finale of our hand-posing symphony! I hope you've had as much fun exploring the intricate dance of digits as I had writing about it. From the psychological nuances to the nitty-gritty of anatomy, mastering the art of hand posing is truly transformative, turning everyday snapshots into emotional epics that speak volumes without uttering a single word.

We've journeyed through the essentials of hand anatomy, dived into the deep waters of emotional and cultural expressions, and even toyed with the shadows and lights to craft the perfect mood. Whether it was tying the knot in bridal photography or capturing the raw energy in street photography, we've covered the gamut, proving that hand posing is a universal skill, essential across all photography genres.

Remember, the heart of this book wasn't just to tweak how you position a pinky or a palm but to ignite a passion for telling more compelling stories through your photos. Every chapter was crafted to not only enhance your technical skills but to inspire you to see hands as powerful tools of communication, capable of adding a profound layer of depth and emotion to your work.

Now, don't let this be the end. Photography, like any art, thrives on continuous learning and practice. Keep experimenting with the poses we've discussed, mix them up, and maybe even break some rules along the way. The true mastery of hand posing comes from the willingness to practice, persist, and patiently evolve your craft.

And hey, why go at it alone? Jump into our vibrant online community where you can share your hand-posing triumphs and tribulations. It's a space to learn from each other, offer feedback, and keep growing. Your unique experiences and insights could be just what another photographer needs to have their 'aha' moment.

I encourage you to use this book as your launchpad for creative exploration. Develop your signature style, one that reflects your unique artistic voice, and let your hands—literally—do the talking. Remember, in the world of photography, your creativity is the only limit.

Thank you sincerely for joining me on this remarkable journey. Writing this book has been a process of discovery and delight, and I hope it has offered you the same, inspiring you to transform not just your photographs but the way you view the world through your lens.

Here's to more expressive, impactful photography, and remember—keep those hands talking and cameras clicking!

Also by Amanda Otis

This photography book series is your ultimate resource for mastering the art and business of photography. Each book is packed with expert insights, practical advice, and inspiring examples to help you grow your skills and succeed in the competitive world of photography. Whether you're just starting out or looking to refine your craft, these guides will support you every step of the way on your photographic journey.

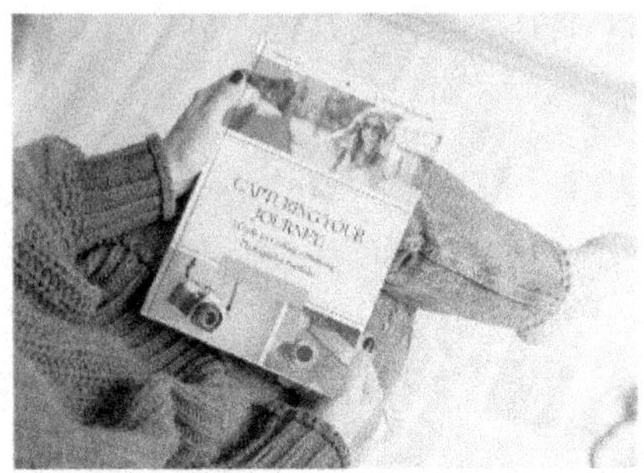

Capturing Your Journey: A Guide to Crafting a Stunning Photography Portfolio (with Helpful Worksheets and 50 Portfolio Building Exercises)

Embark on a transformative journey through the lens with "Capturing Your Journey," a comprehensive guided workbook

designed for photographers aspiring to build their perfect port- folio. This 26-page workbook is a treasure trove of portfolio- building insights, offering a wealth of information and 50 dynamic exercises tailored to help you curate a portfolio that reflects your unique style and vision.

Discover the art of thematic thinking, find your passion, develop depth in your work, and master the art of tight editing with practical exercises that guide you every step of the way. Whether you're a budding photographer or a seasoned pro, this workbook is your companion in honing your craft and creating a portfolio that stands out.

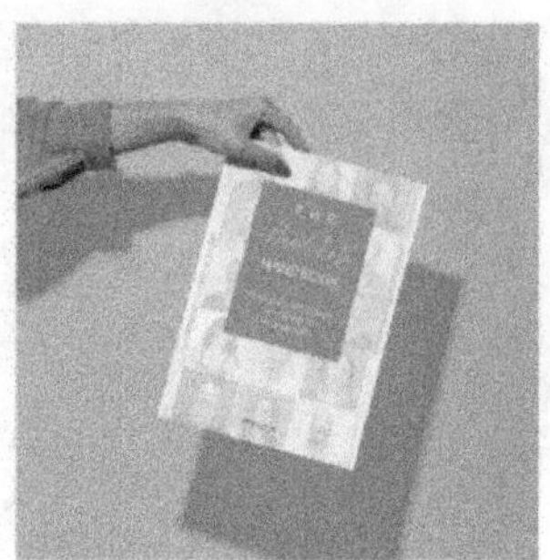

The Headshot Handbook: A Step-by-Step Guide to Headshot Photography

Unlock the secrets to capturing stunning headshots with "The Headshot Handbook: A Step-by- Step Guide to Headshot Photogra- phy." Whether you are a budding photographer or a seasoned professional looking to refine your skills, this comprehensive guide will take you through every aspect of headshot photography.

Inside, you'll find expert advice on selecting the right equipment, mastering lighting techniques, and understanding the importance of angles and expressions. Learn how to create a comfortable environment for your subjects, enabling them to convey their best selves in every shot. The book has practical tips, step-by-step tutorials, and inspiring examples to elevate your photography game.

From corporate professionals to actors and models, "The Headshot Handbook" covers diverse styles and approaches, ensuring you can meet any client's needs. Discover how to perfectly retouch and edit your photos, delivering high-quality results that stand out in today's competitive market.

Transform your headshot photography with this indispensable resource and capture images that leave a lasting impression.

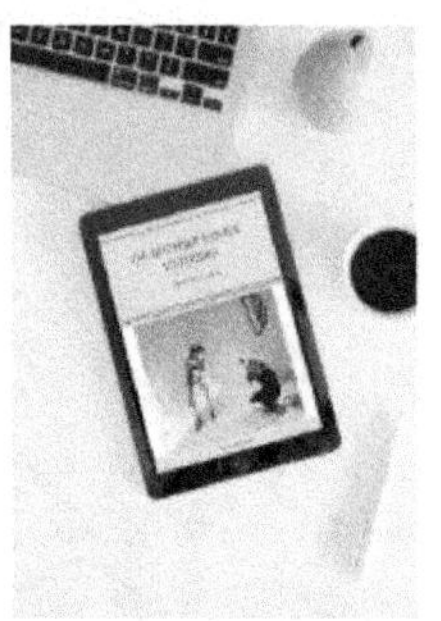

The Beginner's Guide to Posing (with Pictures!)
https://otisdesignboutique.etsy.com/listing/1640479201

This ebook takes your posing game to the next level. Whether you're a seasoned model or a selfie enthusiast, this guide is your go-to resource for striking the perfect pose every time.

What's Inside:

A curated collection of 17 pages featuring various poses suitable for any occasion. From casual to sophisticated, these poses are designed to make you look your best. Visualize each pose with stunning images that showcase the art of posing.

www.ingramcontent.com/pod-product-compliance
Lightning Source LLC
Chambersburg PA
CBHW071309030726
47594CB00002B/359